THE DANCE PROGRAM

A Series of Publications in the Field of Dance and the Related Arts

Volumes in Preparation

Dance Out the Answer, an autobiography, by Madame La Meri, *foreword by John Martin*

On Tap Dancing, by Paul Draper, *edited and compiled by Fran Avallone*

Olga Preobrazhenskaya, a biography, by Elvira Roné, *translated by Fernau Hall*

Ballerina, a biography of Violette Verdy, by Victoria Huckenpahler

The Bournonville School (in four volumes), including music and notation, by Kirsten Ralov, *introduction by Walter Terry*

I Was There, by Walter Terry, *compiled and edited by Andrew Wentink, introduction by Anna Kisselgoff*

The Bennington Years: 1934-1942, a chronology and source book, by Sali Ann Kriegsman

The Art and Practice of Ballet Accompanying (in two volumes), by Elizabeth Sawyer Brady

The Ballet Russe (in four volumes), edited by George Jackson

Imperial Dancer, a biography of Felia Doubrovska, by Victoria Huckenpahler

Antony Tudor, a biography, by Fernau Hall

Dancer's Diary, by Dennis Wayne, *introduction by Joanne Woodward*

Total Education In Ethnic Dance

"Hamsa Rani" (*Swan Queen*) in Indic version of *Swan Lake,* 1944. (Photo: Marcus Blechman)

Total Education In Ethnic Dance

La Meri (Russell Meriwether Hughes)

Foreword by Walter Terry

MARCEL DEKKER, INC.   New York and Basel

Library of Congress Cataloging in Publication Data

Hughes, Russell Meriwether, 1898-
    Total education in ethnic dance.

    (The Dance program; v. 6)
    Bibliography: p.
    Includes index.
    1. Folk Dancing. I. Title. II. Series
GV1743.H83   793.3'1   76-58610
ISBN 0-8247-6519-2

Cover photograph by Images, Cape Cod, Massachusetts
Spine drawings by Cary, West Barnstable, Massachusetts

MARCEL DEKKER, INC.
270 Madison Avenue, New York, New York 10016

Current printing (last digit):
10 9 8 7 6 5 4 3 2 1

PRINTED IN THE UNITED STATES OF AMERICA

To the
Creative Pioneers of the "Golden Age"

Ruth St. Denis
Ted Shawn
La Argentina (Antonia Mercé)
La Argentinita (Encarnación López)
Mei Lan Fang
Katherine Dunham
Uday Shankar

Foreword

My profound admiration for La Meri spans almost the entire length
of my own career as a dance critic—that would be forty years.
During those years, I have relished her dancing, been stirred by her
experimental choreography on ethnic themes, savored her wit and
drunk thirstily of her incredible and endless knowledge of the
world's most deeply rooted dances, ethnic dances.

In this her newest book, I find new facets of her knowledge
giving up-to-the-minute descriptions and appraisals of mankind's
oldest dance experiences. It is a superb book, certainly the finest
book on ethnic dance studies I have ever seen. The book is not a
compilation of steps, patterns, routines. La Meri explores and ex-
plains the immeasurable importance of custom, costume, climate
(even geography) and culture in the generation and flowering of
ethnic dance. Yet she can depart from a worldwide sweep and
focus upon a single part of the body—in this case the spine—and
its unique place in defining ethnic dance characteristics. This chapter on the spine is one of the most brilliant and revealing chapters
of a brilliant and uniquely informative book.

It is unlikely that La Meri knows everything there is to know
about ethnic dance, but until someone proves otherwise, I shan't
believe it!

Walter Terry

v

Preface

For some reason known only to Siva, who orchestrated the Cosmic
Dance of the Universe, all the facets of my career seem to have
been preparing me for the role I have found myself playing during
the past fifty-odd years. It seems I have been cast in the character
of explainer, and it is my destiny to reduce to a common denomi-
nator the complicated techniques and backgrounds of the various
aspects of many dance arts and dance sciences.

I take, for example, the complicated Veda, or scripture, of
Hindu *natya,* which few non-Hindus even try to understand, and
I reduce it slowly and painfully to words of one syllable. I get it
down to such a point that even a babe in arms could begin to
grasp the fundamental idea. I mean by this book to introduce
you to the stalk in the hope that you will climb up and find the
leaves and the blossoms and eventually eat of the very fruit that
will reduce you to the pitiable state in which you find me and
other enthusiastic addicts.

My work has dubious results. I have been told by persons
who are virtual morons that after hearing my lectures they have
found it all so simple it is hardly worth further study . . . so what
is all the shouting about? Well, if these persons do not want to
use their brains, there seems to be no law.

I have been told by persons of respected mentality that the
dance is one art they do not care to have "polluted" by the
mental approach. Perhaps they mean the heart should rule the

vii

head in art expression. But a heart without any head at all is a pathological case. Furthermore, I have been told by those who wish me well that I make a great mistake in explaining these dances before performing them . . . that I thus destroy the glamour. Perhaps they are right. But so what! I think it would be unpardonable of me to put glamour before the need of an understanding of certain arts that God knows, need explaining. The dance sciences of the Oriental countries will survive floods, fires, wars, and pestilences. They have before and they will again. I do not explain to help them, for they scarcely need it. I explain to help *you,* for the dances are as vital a need to humanity as the wheat in the fields. As the Bible says, man does not live by bread alone.

Indeed, I am most humbly honored to be one small instrument in handing down a tradition that may be the ultimate salvation of the human race. Make no mistake. If I seem modest, it is about myself and in no wise extends to the art I practice; for the art of ethnic dance is neither an amusement nor a means of self-expression. As the pundits have taught us, it is a means to taste *rasa* (sentiment or feeling) . . . and to find God.

Writing this book has been no easy task. I have delved into files of lectures and articles that I have written over some fifty years. But beyond that somewhat boring work, I have been driven by the conviction that this is probably my last chance to reach dancers and dance enthusiasts with what I have learned in half a century of dedication. Yet who will read with enough attention to gain from the reading? Today there seems to be little interest in learning from the past. I find it difficult not to rail against the current lack of dedication among young dancers. If they give their audiences as little inspiration as they give their teachers, they are doomed, and American art dance will go into a long hibernation. But in my text I must stick to unchanging truths, and I have tried to leave my personal irritations out of it.

I, myself, did not learn in the scholarly way set forth in this book. Indeed, there were no such books to learn from. I admired —I could almost say adored—and absorbed via pure emotion. Students asking questions brought forth the observations in the following pages. So I must give thanks to all my American students (who are my children and grandchildren), from my first group, the five *Natyas* to my last Ethnic Dance Arts Group, whose talent or orneriness has pushed me to find the answers that comprise this book and that I often first delivered at the top of my well-carrying voice.

The list of Recommended Reading at the back of the book is a mere beginning. Authoritative books on ethnic dance are relatively rare, and many of the best are out of print. In my own library I have approximately five hundred volumes; I have tried to select from these the books that have the most information within their covers.

I am indebted to Walter Terry for the title of this book, although I do not think he is aware that he gave it to me in one of our many conversations over the years I have known him.

I am indebted to William J. Adams, Jr. for the typing of the script, a mean job at best, further complicated by frequent references to the dictionary, for my spelling of English is very questionable.

La Meri

Contents

Illustrations

xiii

Other Works by the Author

Dance As an Art-Form, Principles of the Dance-Art
Gesture Language of the Hindu Dance (*two editions*)
Basic Elements of Dance Composition
Spanish Dancing (*two editions*)

Total Education In Ethnic Dance

one

What Is Ethnic Dance?

The term *ethnic dance* designates all those indigenous dance arts that have grown from popular or typical dance expressions of a particular race. The term came into general usage during the 1940s as a way to differentiate among ballet, modern and ethnic in theater-dance presentations. It was I who introduced the term. I did so with the approbation of such artists as La Argentinita, Antonio, Teiko Ito, and others. It was good, for it gave an added strength to the few of us (in comparison to ballet and modern) who were dedicated to ethnic forms. At that time we who were purists referred to the art dance as ethnologic or ethnological dance. It was a convenient means of quick identification of the ethnic art dance. I must confess we did not succeed in making these latter terms stick. It is a pity, for today there is general confusion in identifying the difference between communal and art dances.

Ethnic dance, then, covers an unwieldy majority of the world's choreography. In the Western Hemisphere the term is useful, since Occidental theater dances are largely ballet or modern. Yet in the Orient the term ethnic dance proves so inexact as to be useless. (It has come to my attention that in the National Art Institute of Java an American woman taught modern dance under the title of Ethnic Dance. Perhaps this is the ultimate explanation of what ethnic dance really is.) In the United States the term Asian dance now covers the bulk of the Eastern Hemisphere. But those of us who are also interested in Spanish, Hawaiian and other Occidental forms cannot use the term Asian without wordy additions. So it seems we shall have to stick with *ethnic* . . . and explain as we go. The title is vague and presents many minor complications . . . as I know very well, since I have worked in its shadow for some thirty years.

Ballet is not ethnic dance because it is the product of the social customs and artistic reflections of differing national cultures. It was built for the edification of the aristocratic, international minority and is not, therefore, a communal expression. The modern dance arts that have grown up in Europe and North America in the last century are not ethnic, because each is the product of one genius and is not a communal cultural expression. Ballet is a product of the cultured classes, from its birth in the court of Catherine de Medici through its growth in the court of Louis XIV to its great glory in the courts of the czars of Russia. Although it has borrowed extensively from folk dance, its roots and motivations are from the European monarchies, and it thus becomes an international rather than a national art expression. Modern (contemporary, or free) dance is the product of the intellectual individual, the iconoclast, the genius . . . from Isadora Duncan through Martha Graham to today's young moderns. Ballet is an art reflecting the mores of a class privileged by birth. Modern dance is a reflection of the current mores as seen through the eyes of a genial individual.

Ethnic dance reflects the unchanging mores of the people of all classes. It was created by and for the people of whatever land or race the dance represents. Ethnic dance arts (or ethnologic dance) are a direct outgrowth of folk expression. In its lineage, then, ethnic dance is the most truly democratic expression of dance, for it carries the aspirations and dreams of all the classes of folk who gave it birth.

There are, of course, examples where the outline blurs a little. Massine choreographed the ballet *The Three-Cornered Hat* to music by Manuel de Falla and a libretto by Martinez Sierra. The story was Spanish, the music based on Spanish themes. But the technique used was largely balletic, and so presented, it comes under the heading of ballet, By contrast Argentinita's staging of the same ballet was ethnic, since concept, techniques, and staging were purely Spanish. The modern, or contemporary, dance, although sometimes enriched by ethnic details, is still the product of the individual artist.

It is my opinion that all ethnologic dance arts are the slow processing of the communal dance. I do not believe that a dance art can be expressive of a certain people unless it is a cross section of that people. Ballet is not ethnic dance because it is the result of Italy, France, Spain, Russia, England . . . and now the United States. As such it cannot fully represent any of the six named. By the same reasoning modern dance is the product of individuals and not of the American people. We cannot hurry the production of an art form as we do the assembly line. I do not doubt that with the passing of the years, nay, of the centuries, the American moderns will have made their contribution to our country's dance. But we cannot afford to disregard the jazz forms. The jitterbug was an exact parallel of the flamenco. Both gitano and rug cutter beat the floor in ecstatic counter rhythms to satisfy an emotional urge, little aware of the effect on those who watched him. One hundred years ago the average cultured Spaniard felt toward the flamenco dance much as many cultured Americans feel toward jazz or rock. But today flamenco is a beloved art and has been fused with Andalusian folk dance to produce the neoclassic dance of Spain. Here lies a lesson that we cannot afford to disregard. For it has always been and will always be the emotional experience of the folk of a race that is the backbone of a country's ethnic dance art. In its finest form ethnic dance is an integral part of the worship, education and everyday life of all classes.

Ethnic dance has several forms or aspects. The first and most basic is the folk dance. The folk, or communal, dance is a dance to be done; a dance in which the joy lies in the doing; and a part of the joy is in the unified purpose that moves a group of persons intent on the same end. Folk dance is the folk, dancing, and you will not see it until you travel to a community of its birth. The

folk dance you see on the stage has already made the transition
into art dance, for it has become dance to be seen. Folk dances
that do not possess a technical terminology, a traditional style, or
a clearly defined school of instruction have not yet made the transition to theater or art dance . . . or, shall we say, ethnic dance.
Understand, then, that all folk dances presented onstage have, in
that presentation, become theater dances and thus a part of the
second main category of ethnic dance . . . the art dance. It is interesting to note that in our own times many folk dances have made
this transition: those of the Ballet Folklorico of Mexico, the
dances of Africa (performed by Pearl Primus, Olatunji, and others),
Peruvian dances (Ballet Peruano), and many others. These dances
remain ethnic only so long as the folk style and basic techniques
are preserved. When the choreographer has recourse to ballet or
strictly modern techniques, the production is no longer ethnic.
Typical costumes and music are not enough to retain the ethnic
essence.

The second main category of ethnic dance is the art dance,
which includes temple and theater dances that, growing out of
folk tradition, carry with them into their highest forms the ideals
and beliefs of the people who gave them birth. Under this heading
fall the highly developed art dances of the Orient, Spanish stage
dances, and theater pieces that use authentic techniques without
recourse to extraneous schools. It includes dances created for
worship, such as Hindu *natya* or the ancient Hawaiian meles
(chants); highly stylized theater dances, such as the Javanese
wayang wong and the Japanese Noh; dances used as social entertainment, such as certain Muslim forms; and communal dances
introduced to the theater relatively recently, such as the Mexican
and flamenco.

The ethnic art dance takes several forms. In its natural habitat the motivation is overlaid by the desire to educate as well as
entertain the spectator. But in transplantation to the stage, the
original motivation, the primal cause, must not be lost, or the
dance will lose its true essence. Brought to the stage, the ethnic
dance arts may take, loosely, any one of five forms: traditional,

4

authentic, creative neoclassic (or renaissance), creative departures, and applied techniques.

The Traditional

Here the performing artist retains the traditional costume, music, techniques, and dance form, or routine. The Kabuki dance-drama is traditional. Cuttings from the Kathakali drama and dance excerpts from other Oriental dance-dramas may be traditional.

The Authentic

The artist uses the traditional costume, music, and techniques but takes certain liberties with the form. For example, a traditional Bharata Natyam item may take forty minutes to execute. Without a native audience this is impossible, so the artist cuts the item down to four or five minutes. Or again, a flamenco dance in its traditional form is improvised on a rhythmic scheme and under immediate emotional pressure. In presenting it on the stage it is necessary more or less to set the routine.

The Creative Neoclassic or Renaissance

Here the scope is broader and more difficult to define. The artist may take liberties with costume, music, and form. Only techniques remain constant. The creative artist stays within tradition in style and motivation. In both the Spanish and Hindu fields the creative dance was originated by individual geniuses. Uday Shankar used Indian themes, costumes, motivation, and technique. His accompanying music, played on Indian instruments, was composed for his ballets and dances. La Argentina used techniques and motivations of Spain, but she was the first Spanish dancer to use the classic music of Spain's great composers. Both these artists started a trend that has become so strong as to be a school.

Creative Departures

A very thin line distinguishes the creative neoclassic from the creative departure. In the departure form costumes are traditional in

5

line, but certain liberties are taken. Techniques remain traditional but may be mixed as to school or handled more freely. The music may be completely alien, but the general aura of motivation is kept intact.

Applied Techniques

Here the traditional techniques are applied to alien themes, music, costume, and motivation. (A category of creative ethnic dance now past is the purely inspirational work of Ruth St. Denis.) Unfortunately many dancers and choreographers think the creative aspect is the easiest part of ethnic art dance. Nothing could be further from the truth. One must always depart from strength, not weakness. To depart from authenticity, one must know authenticity very deeply. One must understand not only the authentic forms but the motivations, else one loses the essence of ethnicity, and the result is a mishmash of schools with no aesthetic value.

There is a category of ethnic dances that, properly speaking, comes under neither folk nor art dance. Although I resent the term, these may be called primitive dances, but only in the sense of original, nonderivative (or primal, first), not in the sense of crude. These are the ritual dances of the Amerinds, certain tribes of southern and central Africa, Australian aborigines, the Nagas of India, and many others. These dances are not folk, because they are not necessarily communal, and the motivation is one of worship or even theatricality. However, the moment these dances are transplanted to our stage they become art dances, so you are not likely to see them in their purity unless you travel to their native soil (or catch them on television). Of the primal dances recently brought to the theater the richest have been various forms of African dance. In the hands of inspired choreographers the black dance has proven itself capable of many emotional shadings, not the least of which are found in the aspects it takes in the Americas—jazz, Brazilian, Caribbean, and such.

There is often great danger in passing from a folk expression to an art form. Emasculation may lie between. The Scottish dances were born as the emotional expression of a bold and war-like people. Not many years ago I saw them danced by the Gordon Highlanders. It was the most thoroughly exciting performance I had ever witnessed. But what of the passage of these dances toward the academicism of artistry? One sees girls of twelve, hung with the medals of past awards, executing reel, fling, and sword dance in virginal ballet slippers, battement-trained toes beating slim calves with careful precision. But is this the Scottish dance? God forbid! For the breath of life has gone out of it, and it has forgotten why it was born!

One day in my Spanish class I suddenly realized that at the earnest badgering of certain of my pupils I had been for some months teaching steps with painful precision, yet all these steps had not led to the execution of a single *copla* of the sevillanas! I tried in an impassioned speech to my gaping students to explain my feelings, my violated principles . . . and I sailed out of the classroom registering the vow that I never again would teach a dance whose very essence lies in its emotional fathering, via the route of precise technique.

For the ethnologic dance is not a product of the mind but of the emotions. Style is its essence, and technique is of purely relative importance. Technique, or body control, must be mastered only because the body must not stand in the way of the soul's expression.

This, then, is ethnic dance—a vast panorama of human expression in its purest form, forever changing and growing, both in its natural habitat and in its transplantation to alien ground. It is a study for one who is at once a scholar, a dancer, and a creator, hence its protagonists are few and deeply dedicated.

In subsequent chapters we shall take up the demands of the study of ethnic dance and the many benefits this study brings.

two

Total Education in Ethnic Dance

To study ethnic dance, whether in one form or in its many manifestations, one must immerse oneself. It is not possible to work only on the physical techniques, for that way the dancer will be a shell, a puppet, a mechanical master of movement. It is the motivating spirit behind a movement that makes it heart-stopping for the watcher. Ethnic dance must be both theatrical and scholarly. The acolyte must study endlessly the background, history, religion, and many other facets of fact and philosophy that gave birth to the dance arts he would make manifest.

Some students are "called" to a specific ethnic form before they begin to dance. For these the lines of background study are relatively clear. But for those who deeply desire to become eclectic ethnic dancers the bulk of background study that confronts them is frightening!

Total education in ethnic dance demands far more than physical control, which, happily, may be obtained through some two thousand hours of studio practice. Other techniques besides the purely physical must be attained before one may be called a well-rounded ethnic dancer.

In 1940 Ruth St. Denis and I founded the school of Natya in New York City. Out of the school grew the Ethnologic Dance Center, which functioned as an academy until 1956. The curriculum of this academy was laid out as a beginning—an introduction

if you will—for the lifelong education of the total ethnic dancer.
I list below the studies demanded in a four-year Artists' Course at
E.D.C.:

1. Physical Techniques: Classes were graded and complete notebooks of terminology demanded (four to six hours daily).
2. History and Culture: Lectures, research, and complete notebooks required.
3. Music: Western—note values, movement to music, dynamics of music translated into physical movement. Eastern—study of Indian *talas* and playing of *tablas.*
4. Writing and Speaking: Articles written and lectures given by graduates.
5. Composition and Choreography: Study of the structure; works presented onstage.
6. Makeup, Costumes, and Production: Graduate students were presented in concert at Carnegie Recital Hall and were required to manage their production and supply their own costumes.
7. Pedagogy: Lectures and notebooks; practical work teaching selected classes under supervision.

Those were only the instruction hours. For those who succeeded add endless practice and study hours. Some students began at 8 A.M. During lunch and supper hours someone was always practicing. When evening classes were over (at 10 P.M.), some students worked until 2 or 3 A.M. (I know, for my living quarters were in this madhouse for several years!)

The foregoing is the basis of study for any and all who would understand the projection of ethnic dance forms. The study, of course, never ends. All one's life one continues to research these backgrounds, and finding a new authoritative book or film (or guru) that can add to one's knowledge is an exciting and wonderful experience.

The acolyte who begins with the study of ethnic dance in eclectic form—that is, one who studies several forms of ethnic dance—need make no clear-cut decision at the incipience of study, for life and his own temperament will generally decide for him which form he will pursue. Each dance art will immeasurably enrich the other. Many of my students have studied all forms and then gone on to a career in one aspect.

Our graduates were few, for a dedication to so arduous a course is rare. But all who graduated have added strength to the ethnic dance in America. Many are excellent performers; most are excellent teachers; some are fine choreographers, writers, and lecturers. Those few who did not stay active in the field have found their lives enriched greatly by the study in depth of ethnic dance.

So the climb is long and arduous. Do not deceive yourself that there are shortcuts. Do not imagine that your teacher can explain to you the basic accents of the *seguiriyas* in a few sentences and that you will then be able to dance it! No, my dear, you must live with it. You must play, endlessly, recordings. You must read and study to try to understand the soul of flamenco, which has produced it (and according to the great Argentinita, you must live at least thirty years), then perhaps you can really dance it. For you do not learn it; you absorb it.

One young student asked, "Why should I learn the basic elements of composition? I just put on the music and dance to it the way I feel!" Well, it's a free country and there is no law to stop you. But dance in its essence is communication, and without words you cannot speak. No one invents the basic laws of air design, floor design, and dramatic design. They are there, so one must be aware of them in order to "speak and speak clearly at all costs" (Ananda K. Coomaraswamy).

Do not imagine that all your learning is done in classes. As for the musician, every lesson must be followed by many hours of practice. From the first lesson progress is dependent on outside practice. Consider for a moment your teacher, who must watch you wallowing in the same technical mistake week after week. Give him a break, kids. Take a few hours off to practice and learn that *adavu* properly . . . and I hope the brilliant result will not give your long-suffering guru a heart attack of surprise!

If you are going into dance to be rich and famous, give it up and sell groceries, for you will make more money feeding the body than feeding the soul. But if you are truly dedicated, *nothing* will turn you from your path. You will find life full to overflowing, and your complaints about debts and harsh critics will be only cocktail-party chitchat.

The protagonist of ethnic dance has a serious role to play. To our audiences we are introducing a unique segment of mankind in a unique moment of the soul's journey. Just as Martha Graham shows us the inner turmoil of Judith, so must the ethnic dancer show the inner peace of the dedicated devadasi or the aristocratic pride of the Spaniard. Like the Oriental we must submerge ourselves in the art and express the primal motivations clearly, fairly, and honestly. We have a trust as sure as that of any diplomat. Let us not betray by false witness.

To achieve truth in the projection of motivations one must work for mental control, for individual imagination is the most powerful means of emotional expression.

The power of the mind over the body is an ancient truth in the East (*vide* yoga). It has been accepted in the West in several forms—Christian Science, mesmerism, types of psychoanalysis, and others. All fine artists achieve a sort of mass hypnosis over an audience. It is true that if you believe something strongly enough, it becomes true.

In eastern dance the dancer's complete identification with the character or mood danced is called the Other Thought.

To achieve mental control (and without mental control there is, surely, no physical control) the western dancer should cut through accepted social (and perhaps artistic) mores to grasp the essential emotional reaction common to all mankind. We must open mind and heart to the expression of emotions that social habits have taught us to abjure. The dancer should believe in the Other Thought and become one with it.

The use of imagination in movement should be taught as definitely as the use of the limbs, for too often in the study of the control of the instrument of expression (the body) the original reason for study (the desire to express oneself physically) is lost, and the student becomes a puppet pulled by the strings of muscular theories. Thus, after several years of technical study, there begins the long, agonizing, and, too often, barren search for the spontaneous joy of expression that first drew the student toward dance. The nurturing of the imagination toward expression should go hand in hand with the preparation of the body for this expression.

1. Concentration on the belief is more effective than concentration on the techniques—i.e., emotional concentration on the space covered covers more space than concentration on the muscular effort to cover space.

2. Motivation and dynamic quality are the raisons d'être of the dance. All other techniques are merely adjuncts of these. (This truth, too, is in common usage in the dances of the East.) With these two present an incomplete technique is overlooked; without them a perfect technique is as if not. It is not through ignorance but through a profound instinct toward the truth of beauty that the general public will accept and love the artist who embodies these qualities. It is not the public but the young dance student (and sometimes the writer on dance) who has put physical acrobatics above motivation and dynamics.

3. Movement in space is in the realm of mental control. The imagination makes one aware of the space within which one moves. One can draw patterns in the air and leave a trail behind as a plane would. One can move through a heavy fog or water in a way that makes these elements exist. One can leap great distances, leaving lakes and forests beneath one. One can even send lines far beyond the limits of one's own anatomy.

4. The ability to isolate emotional levels is mental control. No matter that the whole body is moving; the Other Thought, concentrated on the part of the anatomy that best expresses the mood, will unerringly bring the watcher's eye to it.

5. Rediscover the joy of movement!

Unfortunately the young student only too often is unwilling to attack the simplest problem first, preferring to join immediate battle with what seems most difficult, just as he chafes against training his muscles to respond before he attempts a technical tour de force.

The body is the instrument through which the dancer speaks. He must understand the infinite subtleties of which the anatomy

13

is capable. While strengthening the muscles for the rigors of *taconeo* and *that,* he must also train wrists, neck, and eyes to respond.

Nearly all forms of western dance neglect entirely or make subservient those very parts of the body upon which the East lays greatest stress. Many students of western dance arts overlook the study of the hands, arms, shoulders, neck, and face, leaving the expressive qualities of these entirely to the natural talent of the performer. But the upper body is more expressive than the lower body. Isadors Duncan declared that all expressive movement had its impetus in the solar plexus. François Delsarte, in his study of physical expression, discovered that all spiritual and intellectual movement occurred in the upper parts of the body. The science of Bharata Natyam puts all expressive movement in the arms and hands, the head and upper torso—a theory the entire Orient shares.

Torso: The upper torso should lead and dominate the whole. In the practice that over the years gives physical control the spine and its adjuncts should be exercised as consistently and intelligently as the limbs.

Neck, shoulders, chest, waist, and pelvis should be capable of movement that disturbs no other part of the anatomy.

Oriental dance, more particularly the science of Bharata Natyam, has produced the most complete breakdown of the torso, so a consistent study of the Hindu exercises of these parts is of inestimable value to the dancer.

Arms (hands, wrists, elbows, arm sockets): There should be absolutely no limit to the control of the arms. Muscles and joints should be trained to move any way possible to anatomical structure.

In some types of western dance we have fair control of elbow and arm socket but not of wrist and hand. Yet it is the wrist and hand that stop the air design or send it out to infinity.

The wrist and every joint of every finger should be under control—successions of the wrist and hand; circular, perpendicular, and lateral movements in the wrist; tension and relaxation in the hand (palm and fingers); as well as placement of the fingers.

No part of the anatomy is used as much in everyday living as

14

the hands and face. Why, then, neglect the hands and face in expressive dance?

Feet and Legs (Toes, soles, ankles, knees, leg sockets): The lower limbs generally receive the most attention in the study of western dance (one learns "the steps"). Leg socket and knee are most generally capable of lift, throw, and circular movements. But we neglect the feet and ankles. The contact of the sole and the ground is highly expressive. The foot can, in effect, dance on, under, or above the ground (I speak of emotional effect; by above the ground I do not mean leaps). The foot can caress the earth or strike it in anger or spurn it in flight (or be gingerly unacquainted with it, as is the case of too many dancers).

First comes the training of the body—muscle by muscle, the great and the small, until every shading of movement is alive, every kinetic line etched, every dynamic tone painted—the hair, eyelids, toes, subtle waist and fingertips. This training is forever.

At a certain plateau in the domination of the body begins the second phase of learning: the training of the conscious mind—the knowledge of all things pertaining to the subject, both past and present; the knowledge of sound and cloths; of space and air; of light and dark; and, most of all, of the heart of mankind and your own heart. This training too is forever.

Once again, at a certain plateau in the domination of the body combined with the knowledge of the conscious mind begins the third phase of learning: the training to call at will on the alter ego —the awareness of primal truths; the becoming of another being in another place; the embodiment of an all-consuming passion of another motivation.

Few reach the level of the third phase, for the climb to it is long and arduous, and it is safer never to have begun at all or to have stayed with others on the first or second plateau. For the high, thin winds that blow above the third plateau are filled with danger . . . even the danger of no return. There is loneliness and the fear that rides with loneliness. There is infinite sadness, for one cannot return to the sunshine that lies at the beginning, and perfection is never achieved.

15

Ah, but when at last the veil falls and the ultimate of becoming is reached, however briefly, the soul transcends and becomes one with infinity.

The aspects of the guru must be forever three and forever changing:

1. For the first phase he must have humor and strength as well as patience and faith.
2. For the second he must have knowledge, strength, skill, and sympathy.
3. For the ultimate, or third, phase he must have courage, understanding, imagination, and mysticism.

All know him as he is in the first phase; some know him as he is in the second phase; but he is blessed if even *one* should know him in the third phase.

I have written and taught in the first, popular phase until I am weary of forever starting over. In the second, erudite phase I have written until I despair of its efficacy. In the third phase I have written little, and only for myself, for I have never found an acolyte who could scale the heights.

But I have known these heights, and I am content.

three

Why Study Ethnic Dance?

It may well be asked of you, "Why do you study ethnic dance?"
For those dedicated to the performance of ethnic dance the answer
is simple enough—the performance itself. But there are other
profits to be gained from this study. The answer to the question
must be twofold.

First, "for physical control and enrichment." The ethnic
dance in all its forms embodies movements that do no violence to
the body structure. It does not demand that tendons be stretched
so that bones will swing in their sockets to an unnatural angle or
that sinews be stretched beyond natural scope. For this reason
ethnic dance can be practiced by a soft-boned child in perfect
safety and is within the physical possibility of an untrained body
of fifty.

It builds the muscles with great subtlety and without undue
strain. Indeed, many youngsters who feel that they have not
really danced unless they leave class sweaty and sore are deluded
into believing that certain forms of ethnic dance are just too easy
to be bothered with. But the difficulties are subtle, not sweaty.
You are threading a needle, not driving a pole into the earth.

If basic exercises are done correctly and conscientiously, the
body control improves much faster than the student realizes. If
you have tried hatha-yoga, you know how quickly, yet how sub-
tly, the body responds to it. Hindu dance techniques, based on

each and every articulation, are as quick and subtle as yoga. These two sciences go hand in hand and can bring about a physical control that is almost miraculous.

The second answer to the question is "for mental enrichment." In ethnic dance we have several thousand years of experience from which to draw. The study of its manifold dance movements from physiological, psychological, and sociological standpoints is tremendously rewarding.

In my years of teaching I have had in my classes ethnologists, anthropologists, linguists, humanitarians, musicians, and psychologists. All these specialists in other fields knew that ethnic dance offers a key to open many doors in their own work, for all folk arts reflect the aspirations and mores of that folk, and the dance arts are a sublimation of the everyday lives of the people. Their study brings a deep personal understanding and a humanitarianism where egocentricity cannot live: not "How do I feel?" but "How does the human race, to which I belong, feel?"

To use ethnic techniques properly one must understand something of the backgrounds that gave them birth. Indeed, it is practically inevitable that the student of ethnic dance becomes interested in the cultural backgrounds of the dance. However superficial the study of movement may be, questioning the why for certain movements will plague the student until he finds himself stimulated into some research. Through these studies the student breaks down the barriers of mental habit to find a far broader aesthetic knowledge. He finds that the basic emotions of all mankind are identical and that these emotions are expressed differently only because the mores of the folk have brought about a superficial difference in physical movement. Through a study of the philosophy, religion, and way of life of alien peoples we can, given an open mind, understand the deep, underlying brotherhood of man, and this will inevitably lead to tolerance, understanding, and sympathy.

The dance is so close to sincere human expression. It is so direct and simple in its appeal. It reaches so far and expresses so much. It is an unfailing barometer of the temperament of a folk. Through it one may understand the spiritual aspirations of a race.

18

The study of ethnic dance broadens the scope of the body, mind, and heart and gives to its protagonist a healthy mind in a healthy body.

In all its aspects ethnic dance makes a very clear differentiation between male and female. After the first basic lessons male and female techniques differ widely; separate classes are almost necessary. Indeed, certain dances in their entirety are taboo for women and others for men. Certain movements and styles always belong exclusively to a given sex.

For the specialist in ballet or modern dance the study of one or more ethnic forms brings manifold benefits. Eminent teachers of ballet have sent their students to me for study in Spanish dance to give them a straight back and beautiful arm carriage. Many young ballet dancers have achieved solos in certain ballets because of their ability to play castanets.

For the creative or modern dancer ethnic forms offer great physical enrichment. The body has endless means of expression of which the creative modern dancer is often only half aware. To make the instrument of expression, the body, complete, one should learn what older lands have long ago learned of physical expression. In variety of pure physical movement the modern dance can borrow a great deal from established ethnic dance arts and be greatly enriched thereby.

The archaic motivations of all forms of ethnic dance can be gathered under five headings: worship, education, health, work (or war), and mating. For example, Hindu dance began thousands of years ago as an adjunct of formal worship. Even as late as forty years ago it was still associated only with religious festivals.

In this country only recently has there been a state-wide movement to incorporate dance into the church service, and some people think this is a new development. Yet Ruth St. Denis worked for many years on an American worship dance. Inspired by the "talking hands" of India, she was well into, but never finished, a vocabulary of hand gestures that was purely American.

The art dance has also only recently been accepted in our higher-education institutes. Yet for many centuries it has been the

19

means of education in other lands. Through it are taught the history, religion, literature, and mores of a folk.

Dance has long been used as a road to better health. The Maoris have used dance as therapy for centures. Yet only now are we beginning to recognize the miraculous healing inherent therein. (Let us draw the veil over our gropings toward health exercises prevalent at the beginning of this century.)

For many centures dance has been used as psychological preparation for disagreeable work. The Maoris, the tribes of Africa, and the American Indians employed dance as a means of exciting the warrior toward war, although this too had its religious aspect insofar as the dance was also an invocation for victory.

Among agrarian peoples dance is used to celebrate the harvest. This too had its beginnings in remote times. In many cases the need for these dances has passed, but the dance lingers on.

The last-named motivation for dance, mating, was the primal cause, for before man stood, the animals danced in the mating season. This remains the most constant of motivations. Mankind may change his religion, his mores, and his need for violence, but sex is always with us!

So we find that dance has always been important to mankind . . . so important that we of the United States should feel primitive in our gropings after truth and recognition. But it is heartening to find that we are not blazing a new trail to the popularization of the dance, and we can learn much by studying the well-worn paths of other peoples.

There are those of us whose motivation for dance is theater. This is what makes us ethnic dancers and not folk dancers. Here we have a strong kinship to ballet and modern dance, both of which were born to theater. But in transplanting ethnic forms to the stage we cannot overlook the primal motivations or we are lost. The ancient religious motivation of Hindu dance gives it forever a spiritual remoteness from the immediate world. Odori onstage must not lose the gay spontaneity of its street origins. The hula must always reflect its bucolic beginnings and evoke waterfalls, flowers, sea, and sand. If you instinctively do not like a certain ethnic-dance performer, it is inevitable that the reason is the loss of the primal motivation.

It is interesting to observe that ethnic dance in all its aspects —although many of these aspects were not theater-born—has a tremendous audience impact. All of us who are ethnic dancers are "riding" on the appeal of the art we practice. An audience with an open mind welcomes ethnic dance with enthusiasm. Even done badly, ethnic dance gets over. Discounting the aesthetics, ballet has a sort of snob appeal, while modern dance has a superintellectual appeal. But for the general public ethnic dance wins in a walkaway. They will give you reasons why they like it. They will say, "The costumes are so beautiful." But they do not go to see these same costumes in a museum! As for the music, when we move to the East, they find the music "dreadful." Techniques they do not understand at all. What they are responding to, although, of course, they don't know it, is the underlying motivation of sincere primal causes. Why is Spanish dance so popular (and always has been)? Because it presents an uninhibited expression of basic emotions with an honesty we wish we could achieve. And Indian dance? Because it invokes a god of sublimated human attributes.

The protagonist of ethnic dance has a serious role to play. We must depict the folk of a race clearly, honestly, fairly: the dignity of Spain, the joyousness of Hawaii, the oneness with Brahman of India. We are showing the universality of human emotion by means of multiform rhythmic expression.

When will we learn that man does not live by bread alone? Or by a fat bank account, chain stores, steam heat and plumbing! I am talking about living, which is a state that exists only in you . . . in your soul and mind.

What has this to do with dancing? Everything. Art is the food of the soul, the bread of real existence. And of all the arts, dance, and more particularly ethnic dance, is closest to those sentiments and moods that can never be put into words. We Americans are so poor in cultural backgrounds, and there is so much we can learn in art and philosophy from other, older peoples. "Why from dancing? Why not from books?" you may ask. Because dancing is so much more honest . . . and so much more pleasant. It isn't the only way to get acquainted, but it is one of the best ways.

For the amateur student of ethnic dance the onus of honest presentation of racial motivations is not so heavy, for he is speaking to a friendly, local audience. For the professional dancer who carries the message to alien soils the burden is heavy indeed. He must submerge himself in his art and intuitively grasp and interpret original causes. He must serve his art, not be served by it. For art in its highest sense serves nobody; you get out of it exactly what you put into it. You cannot bargain with art, with love, or with God. If you are truly dedicated, you will give little or no thought to the material gains, nor will you be tortured by the devils of envy.

For the professional dancer who wishes to perform an alien art background studies are a must. Should an American wish to perform Spanish dance, there are only two sure ways. One is to spend his formative years in Spain (the years between the ages of eight and twenty), and the other is to study and read endlessly—the history, art, music, literature, and all else that is available.

In the Orient they have understood the value of the dance. "A king can be judged by the state of the dancing during his reign." In India, Nataraj creates the rhythmic universe through the dance. In Java only the most cultured persons may teach the dance.

In a world hourly growing smaller it behooves us as human beings to understand something of the peoples of this rapidly shrinking world. The student of ethnic dance has the shortest possible cut to the understanding of alien peoples, for he can learn to know them without climbing the barrier of language. He can know them through movement. For it must always be remembered that ethnic dance is the direct and honest expression of the people who gave it birth. Thus by trying to move as they move we understand them better. Knowing that basic emotional motivation is the same all over the world—happiness, self-preservation, the search for God— we find what paths of beauty these alien peoples take to achieve these universal goals.

When the dancer has understood that basic emotions are the same in all mankind—when he has absorbed the philosophy, religion, mores—he will become as sensitive to emotional projection as the native.

There are subtleties of body control that are an integral part of certain ethnic techniques and as techniques are unique to that form. The study of these techniques will give the dancer a whole new vocabulary of body expression. For example:

The delicate subtlety of emotional expression in Japanese dance
The steady dynamic flow of Javanese dance
The spiral line of Spanish dance
The isolated controls of Indian dance
The impressive ground contacts of the Amerind, flamenco, Kathak, and
    many others

I call these body controls (and others like them) the within techniques of ethnic dance. Only too often the usage of these within techniques is left to the immediate genius of the performing artist. Yet the conscious study of them will immeasurably enrich the body vocabulary of the creative dancer. Walter Terry has called these within techniques "the special movement facilities of many peoples, presented not as ethnic material but as additional disciplines for the total dance."

The end result of the study of within techniques is quality of body expression.

Quality is the most important element of any type of dance. Yet only too often in studying dance one learns simply the steps, gestures, outer techniques, assuming that quality is a prerogative of the native or of the rare artist who can catch quality by osmosis. I believe that quality can be awakened and in some cases taught. It is true that the majority of the elements listed here are found, at one time or another, in all fine dancing. Therefore students of any type of dance can use this work for their own betterment. I also believe quality to be of particular value to the choreographer who wishes to portray the mood or feeling of an ethnic theme without using the more obvious techniques, such as *taconeo* or a fast *sundari*. For example, there is currently a good deal of misunderstanding about Spanish dance, and I have become very irritated by the use of certain clichés that frankly are most un-Spanish—the exag-

23

gerated shrug of the shoulder and toss of the head or the fierce scowl. We want quality, not "españolismo." It distresses me to see the young student becoming increasingly preoccupied with "applause-jerking" acrobatics at the sacrifice of quality.

In many Oriental lands the delicate nuances are taught as a technique. One evening at a performance of Kabuki will amply prove my point. But the West has not recognized the profound truth of Coomaraswamy's statement, "When the curtain rises, it is too late to begin the making of a new work of art."

We must, then, isolate and clarify certain essences of physical movement that are inherent in a given ethnic dance form. These within techniques are applicable to any form of dance art, and I believe they can be taught. We need only to select those elements that are, or should be, universal.

Beginning with the feet, the student should be taught to feel the ground—with the balls of the toes, the ball of the foot, and the heel. The foot should be expressive in itself. The knees should feel the weight of the body and of the emotion motivating the movement. The thigh and calf should feel the displacement of space, aware of the air through which the limb is moved.

The arms too must feel the displacement of space as well as their relationship to the all-important torso and the need to express the emotions within that torso.

The hand, that marvelously contrived mechanism that is itself the main repository of the sense of touch, should be trained toward the full expression of emotion. (How neglected the hand is in western schools of dance! Yet, more than the face, it is the thermometry of emotion. It is the mechanism of all materialized creative work, from the building of a house to the writing of a book. Painters and sculptors have long recognized the importance of the hand as the vehicle of emotion. Why has western dance lagged so far behind?)

The face, above all the eyes, should be taught to mirror the emotions. In the small area of the face can be seen not only the feelings of the moment but the emotions of all past life. Why, then, must the dancer eschew these strongest mirrors of feeling—the face and the hands?

In the trunk of the body is the mainspring of all movement. The dancer should learn to feel the emotional expression of the spine and control it as easily as he does his limbs. He must also learn to feel the emotional rhythms of breath, which is the basic reaction to emotion. The head and neck must also be made to be expressive in dance as they are in nature, responding to feeling and mood. (It is amazing how few dancers can control their necks!) As the body is being trained . . . perhaps I should say "untrained," since the aim is to take away from the body the confinement of clichés imposed upon it by foolish clothes and shoes and equally foolish social mores. Let us say instead as the body is being freed, so must the mind be freed, so that the imagination can work spontaneously and the dancer can find himself. Surely we are not a nation of sheep that must all jump over the same fence in the same way! Each individual is individual, and the only feeling worth expressing is that which is inherently his own. Let me add that all great dancers, in whatever school they have studied, have held on to their means of personal expression throughout their years of study. I have no more quarrel with ballet or modern dance than I have with the ethnic schools. I am convinced that a study of the within techniques would be a help and never a hindrance to students of any school.

The richest mine of within techniques is the classic dance of India. It is an art with about three thousand years of tradition behind it, and it was created by a folk intent upon the workings of the inner man. Every possible physical response to emotion has been explored, isolated, and docketed. Here we find the deliberate and involuntary expressions of the face and hands deeply understood and technically taught. This is "reality" in its truest sense, for the face and hands betray to the watcher both the immediate emotion and the emotions that have formed our lives. I do not mean by this that every dancer should master the thirty-four basic *hasta mudras,* but the *hasta prana* (the "lives" of the hands) should be a part of his technique.

25

Hasta prana:	fingers curled inward (*kuncita*)
	fingers turned backward (*prerita*)
	hand revolving (*recita*)
	palm turned down (*apavestita*)
	palm turned up (*udvestita*)
	hands fluttering (*punkhita*)
	turned back (*vyavrtta*)
	serpentine movements (*bhujanga*)
	fingers relaxed or separated (*prasarana*)

There are many other items of within techniques, drawn from the dances of Spain, Java, Japan, Hawaii, and others. There are the attacks—the "grace notes" before the movement. There is movement on breath—the slow intake and the quick outgo, or the opposite. There is concentric spiral, isolated control, and many other elements of dynamic expressive control. We must not underestimate the importance of the joints and must understand the emotional levels they express, especially the wrists, fingers, elbows, and shoulders. We must understand physically, mentally, and emotionally the basis of, for example, a sensual movement and at once know that this can be made subservient to, say, the intellectual expression. We must try to command the illusory subtlety inherent in eastern dance, often projected through the delicate follow-through of the eyes and head. Indeed, the training of the head and neck is of utmost importance. Above all, let us return to the other thought—the strength of the imagination and the dancer's belief in the emotional undercurrent of what he does. The performer should know the power of his own belief on the watcher. Nor should he underestimate the power of his own feeling—feeling with his feet the substance he walks upon, feeling the air his body displaces, physically feeling the muscle a given emotion has provoked to movement. We should know and be able to give the relaxation of Hawaii or the tension of Spain.

The foot should be expressive in itself. Let us move the ankle in all possible ways. Let us spread and relax the toes and lift the arch with or without the toes pointed. And above all, let us learn that the sole of the foot can be as expressive as the palm of the hand.

Knees should be locked or loosened at will as a means of emotional expression. Tension is strong, and the pull back to the center of self is in contrast to the push out into space.

All leg movements begin in the hip socket. The thigh can be strong as in East Indian dance or sensual as in Spanish dance. The leg can be thrown from the hip socket as in a kick or merely placed in space.

All movement begins emotionally in the torso. All true successions originate in the torso. Without the spine line no ethnic characterization is possible and no emotional mood complete (see chapter seven). For study we may divide the torso into five sections: the spine, shoulders, waist, hips, and chest, or rib cage. The shoulders are the thermometer of passion and sensibility. The waist can be treated as a sort of joint that separates the emotional chest from the vital pelvis. The chest is expressive in itself. It is also the seat of breathing, which is of great importance in expressive movement. "There is the convulsive, deep breathing of effort or violent emotion; the irregularities of breath in fear and agitation; the shallow, quick breathing of suffering or recovery after effort; the long expiration of breath, which shows the need of ridding the body of poisonous gases and may be used to indicate the result of great tension or relief after tension."*

All torso control should be so complete that understatement is possible. The dance that puts great emphasis on the legs indicates a strong vitality but not a spiritual or thoughtful motivation. The elbows are the thermometer of the will. They draw in for humility and thrust out for arrogance. No part of the body is more obviously indicative of lack of self-confidence than drooping elbows.

Next to the face the hands and wrists are the most expressive parts of the body. Strength, or the lack of it, is shown in the hands and wrists. The wrist is the thermometer of vital force, as witness the curling wrist of the flamenco dancer. The thumb is vital; watch the thumb of the male and female Japanese dancer. I am endlessly

*Delsarte, quoted in *Every Little Movement,* Pittsfield, Mass., Eagle Press, 1954, page 959.

fascinated with expressive wrists and remain far less impressed with the leaps of Nureyev than with his strong, expressive wrists.

Not only immediate moods and emotions but all one's character is reflected in the expression of the face and the carriage of the neck. Indian dramaturgy states that "the heart follows the eye." In chapter ten I have listed the facial expressions as given in the *Natya Sastra*. Delsarte has also made exhaustive studies of facial expression and has listed 405 combinations of the eyes and brows and 98 necks and state that the mouth combined with these runs into the hundreds of thousands. Surely it behooves the dancer to work with these studies in order to bring to full flower his natural facial expression.

The isolated controls prevalent in Indian, Javanese and other types of eastern dance will also enrich the dancer. He will gain the ability to control any part of the body irrespective of what movements other parts of the body may be making—to flip a scarf in staccato while the body is moving in smooth legato. He will use the body not as a unit but as separate parts of a whole.

From Javanese dance we may learn the strength of dynamic flow and space displacement—the unceasing push through space without rise or fall in strength of movement. Before one limb comes to rest the other must begin to move. Dynamic flow is the most conscious use of space displacement, which is the physical consciousness of the space displaced by movement.

Spiral and concentric movements are clearest seen in Spanish dance. Here all movements go out from the center (the torso) to curve back into the center; and there is more strength in the "return" than in the outward movement. If a limb is lifted, there is an almost visible "pull" to bring it back to the central core. The spiral may either rise or fall, but it always curves around the center. Both spiral and concentric movement are highly sensuous and egocentric.

Attack and impetus should be present in all types of dance, but in several forms of ethnic dance these are choreographed and become a technique in themselves. An attack may be either oppositional or circular. In the oppositional attack, if the movement is upward, the attack will be downward, and vice versa. In its understated form the attack should not have a full beat but only a grace note in time. This is not to be confused with the staccato attack, which is sharp attack to a given movement. Oppositional attack may be used in any part of the body and gives added strength to the movement it precedes. Circular attack is a circling of the joint before the movement. Like the oppositional, it is only a grace note in time. It is most effective in the wrists, although it can be used in the elbows, neck, hip, and knee. For example, oppositional (or circular) attack can be used by the wrist in starting an arm movement.

Many other elements of movement quality that would enrich the technique of any dancer are prevalent in certain ethnic dance arts: the architectural form, the drawn and implied lines, within-body dynamic contrast, controlled tensions. Over all is the necessity for the Other Thought.

During my years of "retirement" I pondered a good deal on these within techniques and became convinced that a whole new school of dance movement could be built thereon. I gave a one-week workshop on these techniques that was attended by a small group of dancers—some teachers and some advanced students proficient in modern-dance techniques. Alas! I found that the only dancer who could apply these within techniques to free movement was Rebecca Harris, who already had many years of ethnic dance study behind her! I still think this study is a rich mine, but it would take many years of work on the part of both teacher and student, and many years I do not have left!

four

Creative Ethnic Dance

There is a careless idea, too often accepted, that ethnic dance is a copy and in no wise creative in itself. We have been conditioned to believe that both ballet and modern dance, but not ethnic forms, are creative. First let us briefly analyze the elements of ballet. The choreography is formed with the *enchaînements*—the combinations, if you will—of a set of techniques taught in the classroom. In a story ballet pure dance items—*pas seul, pas de deux,* variations—alternate with the pantomimic passages that tell the story. In the early days the music was written for the choreography. The composer and choreographer were the basic creators in the work, and the dancers brought to it their own creativity of style, dynamics, and dramatic personality. In treating music already written, the choreographer becomes the sole creater.

In modern dance it is much the same. True, the choreographer may create entirely new movements that may not depend on class-learned combinations. But again, the choreographer (and composer) is the creative one, not the dancer. By this statement I do not mean to denigrate the work of such figures as Martha Graham, who has created a whole new system of motivation in physical movement, nor the equally creative work of such figures as Antony Tudor, who has brought a new dimension to the ballet *enchaîne-ments.* I wish to show the creativity in any dance form which exists equally strongly in ethnic forms as in ballet and modern dance.

31

Karanas and *adavus* (*enchaînements*) have existed for many centuries and have been added to by eminent *nattuvanars* (dance scholars). Uday Shankar stands as tall in creative movement as any figure in modern dance.

Creativity in any dance form, then consists of

The performer's immediate interpretation
The choreographer's overall composition
The pioneering of adaptations
The creation of movements and motivations.

In ethnic dance consider the traditional routines, i.e., those dances that are authentic in every detail of step sequence, style, costume, music, makeup. This is the scholarly dance. Behind it lie centuries of intellectual and spiritual study. Yet not all traditional dances are forever unchangeable in the sequence of steps and combinations. A *tillana* performed by one Indian dancer is not necessarily identical to that of another Indian dancer. Certain *adavus* are, to be sure, always present, but the dance in its entirety is not identical. Each guru-choreographer has treated the *tillana* form in a different way. Furthermore, the dance becomes creative via the physical attributes and spiritual approach of the artist-dancer. The routine as such is merely a vehicle for the soul of the artist.

Other classic ethnic-dance forms are even more definitely a vehicle for the dancer's creativity. In flamenco only a rather loose rhythmic structure must be adhered to; therefore every flamenco dance is creative . . . in its purest form it is created "on the hoof." Perhaps this is dance creativity at its height—the spontaneous, immediate creation of emotional expression through movement, restricted only by style and rhythm.

The Arabic solo is even less restricted, for given a rhythm and a basic motivation, the Arabic dancer, like the flamenco dancer, will surely change her "routine" at every performance. So, in many ethnic forms there is immediate creativity within the traditional forms, and in all forms there is the creativity of the performer's interpretation of the basic motivation.

The translocation of the communal folk dance to the theater stage is a specialized creative work. The choreographer must have a full knowledge of the earliest motivation and subsequent motivational transmutations. Clinging to the motivation, the choreographer must use the correct music and traditional steps and formation, yet all must have theatrical appeal. The technical equipment of the dancers must be adequate to perform as every native folk dancer has dreamed himself dancing.

Many native companies have staged brilliant concerts using entirely the folk dances of their respective peoples: the Ballet Folklorico of Mexico, the Bayaxihan of the Philippines, the Moiseyev Dance Company of Russia, and a host of others. Choreography for the folk ballet is, obviously, as creative as choreography for classical ballet. The choreographer must know the strict vocabulary of movement and mount these movements on floor and air designs based on the folkways. But the dramatic design must be pure theater. There are four practical elements to be considered. First is the timing, or the dramatic length, of the number. Second is choice of movement, which should always be selected from the traditional. (I am against the Amerind solo that uses balletic leaps. The earth is too much a part of the soul of the Indian for him to spurn it with such folderols.) Third, the choreography must be built on a carefully considered dramatic design. Last, and most important, the characterization of the folk represented must be true. It is unforgivably insulting to misrepresent the basic character of a folk.

With regard to traditional dance-dramas, some that were born and bred for spectacle in their country of origin have been brought to American stages without losing an iota of authenticity. But even these have been selected and cut in the interests of western theater habits. We are not geared to watch the Kathakali drama or the Chinese opera all night, for we are ignorant of the motivating traditions; besides, we are a nation in a hurry. So even here, creative programming becomes a necessity in the transplanting of a pure theater form.

The renaissance form of ethnic dance is entirely creative. It

33

is a within-the-frame creation; that is, all elements are traditional and/or authentic, but the sum total is a pure creation of the artist-choreographer. As an example, let us consider the matchless works of Uday Shankar. His motivations were entirely East Indian—god legends, legendary dances, folk themes and festivals. Music was written for Shankar's creations by an Indian composer and musician, Vishnudass Shirali. Costumes were traditional in style and line. Techniques, though basically East Indian, were pulled from various schools, and many movement patterns were created from ancient paintings and sculptures. The end result was breathtaking—one of the most beautiful forms of Indian dance. It is a great loss that so few artists have worked within this field. True, it must be almost a teamwork between choreographer and composer to realize the full potential. Admittedly, it takes a very special genius to create such works, yet it is perhaps also necessary that a certain preparation be present to open the mind and heart to a freer way. Shankar began his dancing career performing a Krishna-Radha ballet with Anna Pavolva, and Shirali was a graduate student of western music in Paris. It is conceivable that these experiences gave each of these creators a more liberated approach to their native arts. Other Indian choreographers worked in this renaissance style. Rabindranath Tagore staged his own plays with the pupils of his college at Santiniketan, using dances and movement in a somewhat free style. When I saw this company in 1937, the technique of the dancers was Manipuri, but traditional *chalis* were freely used. Ram Gopal created several solos on Indian themes with mixed Indian techniques. In India several fine artists have worked in this medium: Ragini Devi, Menaka, Hima Devi, and others. Strangely enough, in the mother country these creative works have not always been given full acclaim, for the majority of Indian dance enthusiasts prefer the classical forms. (This is an old and sadly repetitious story; the prophet is not without honor save in his own country. St. Denis and Duncan had to leave the United States to be recognized.)

No less creative was La Argentinita's work with folk themes. Using traditional music and costumes, this great creative artist set the relatively few traditional steps into a form called the *bosquejo* —a little character sketch. This character sketch was no easy way out, for it necessitated a thorough understanding of the psychology and mores of each section of Spain. Long ago the aficionado of Spanish dance grew tired of and a little insulted at the stage dancer interpreting the folk as perennially oafish and awkward. Also, La Argentinita's work to Ravel's *Bolero* was a matchless creation. Dividing the composer's work into three parts, she treated the first with classic *escuela bolero,* the second with flamenco, and the third with neoclassic. Each section was handled with a deep knowledge of rhythm and style, and the whole work displayed the wide, almost historical, range of the bolero rhythm. Let us hope this great work will be captured on film before the few who danced in the original production are no longer with us. (So much has been lost that films might have captured! Would not La Argentina be more worth our present contemplation than Hitler?)

Indeed, Ravel's *Bolero* has triggered the inspiration of many creative choreographers. I have used the shortened version as a solo, as has Anton Dolin, while the full-length composition has been staged brilliantly by Maurice Béjart with forty men and one woman and by Florence Rogge at Radio City Music Hall "with a cast of thousands."

Both Katherine Dunham and Jean-Léon Destiné created fine works on Caribbean themes during the "golden age" of creative ethnic dance. Roberto Iglesias and Luisillo worked brilliantly in this idiom. And there have been others who followed the pioneers in the creating of works based on a full knowledge of traditions and a deep feeling for the art handled; for such works require a long preparation in the traditional dance and an inborn understanding of primordial motivations.

A facet of creating new movements and motivations is present in the ethnic dance departure. What we of the ethnic field call a departure is an original work that employs selected elements of a classical ethnic technique in new ways. The elements of authenticity in ethnic dance arts are: choreographic form; character and/or style; costume; music; traditional combinations; motivation and mood; speed and dynamics; inner (or motivational) dynamics; size of air and floor designs; body techniques.

An ethnic departure should partake of only those elements that are peculiarly suited to the selected motivation. This appropriateness is, obviously, the choice of the creator of the work, and the strength of his choice is dependent upon the clarity of his understanding of his motivation and his knowledge of the classical form from which he departs. In this, as in other creative works, it is necessary for the creator to have an honest emotional conviction, not just an intellectual ambition. To create a departure demands a particular talent plus a complete absorption of the traditional and authentic. Given these two, the artist may judge, independently of authentic motivation, what the style of the technique conveys to his emotions through his body. Thus the movement of the body may suggest the mood, as opposed to creating in free movement, where the mood should suggest the movement of the body.

Some of the earliest departures in this country will serve excellently as examples of choice of authentic elements. The late Jack Cole set to swing music the classical *adavus* of Bharata Natyam. The traditional choreographic form was used sparingly; costumes were modified from the classical; speed and dynamics were somewhat exaggerated. Obviously Mr. Cole's departures were based on the rhythmic kinship between the traditional cross rhythms of the authentic dance form and the equally insistent cross rhythms in the American popular music. The result was entirely acceptable to all but the most priggish of traditionalists.

Carmelita Maracci, an extraordinarily creative artist, departed from Spanish dance techniques, of which she was a mistress. Her works probed the deep inner soul of the Spaniard. Costume and music were modified for mood-motivation. Movement was found not in traditional steps but in this mood-motivation. Indeed, this mood-motivation was so strong that all else became its servant. None but the true cognoscenti were enthused about her work, and many of her watchers muttered that what she was doing was not really Spanish. But we know by now that if an artist takes a giant step forward, the understanding of the public is left far, far behind.

I myself did a number of departures in the forties. The *Gesture Songs, Swan Lake,* and *Bach-Bharata* achieved some success (see chapter five), and a later work, *Drishyakava,* to *The Seasons* of Vivaldi (choreographed in 1953) was well received. In all these works the main departures were the use of western music and the mood-motivation of the composition. Thus far both public and critic understood and applauded. But in 1960 I went a step too far.

For quite some time I had been increasingly interested in the within techniques (see chapter three) inherent in ethnic dance forms. In 1958 I made a series of short solos embodying the within techniques of certain ethnic forms to selected short pieces by western composers. These pieces, performed in a noncommittal white crepe costume, were: *Early Winter* (the gentle understatement inherent in Japanese dance), *Incantation* (the strong, ritualistic form of East Indian), *Sea Walk* (the floating surge of Javanese dance), *Life Boat* (the rhythmic insistence of Hawaiian dance), *Spiral Flight* (the rising spiral of Spanish dance). I performed these dances at Jacob's Pillow, and they were received pleasantly enough.

Two years later, still enthusiastic about this within-technique discovery, I created a group of works with myself and four dancers (two male and two female), which I presented at the Pillow. The music was written by Frederick Bristol, who played for our performances. Titled *Escape,* the work consisted of five movements:

1. "Through Work" (the strong, repetitious movements of Bharata Natyam)
2. "Through Play" (the light, contrasting movements of Thai dance)
3. "Through Self-control" (the controlled, understated movements of feminine Japanese dance)
4. "Through Sublimation" (the hypnotic surge of Javanese dance)
5. "Through Defiance" (the self-sufficient pride in Spanish dance)

In the mind of the public I was associated solely with the authentic and traditional, so no one had the vaguest idea what I was up to, and the work died quietly on the Pillow stage.

The moral is that in making a departure, one can sometimes depart so far ahead of the bandwagon that no one knows one is in the parade.

More successful with audiences were the *Gesture Songs* I had created about 1942. Departing from the traditional Indian form of interpreting through gesture and facial expression a song of divine praise (*sloka*), I danced three sacred songs ("Eli, Eli," "Holy, Holy, Holy," and "The Creation") in a black gown and, in accordance with tradition, with a minimum of body movement and floor design. The success of these numbers proved the universality of worship motivation.

Later on I moved into the secular form (*padam*) and danced many popular American songs with Hindu gestures. A study of American Indian sign language also yielded a new field of expression, although songs with Amerind themes were harder to find.

To recap the creative elements in dance as applied to ethnic forms:

The performer's immediate interpretation: Nothing could be more immediately creative than Balasaraswati's rendition of a *sloka,* a *varnam,* or a *padam,* in which she sings as well as gestures. All are created on immediate inspiration. Or the late Carmen Amaya's flamenco items, which were also the fruit of the instant's mood and feeling. But even in a dance with a previously set routine it needs only a little rapprochement in the watcher to acknowledge the personal interpretation in an *alarippu* as danced by Bhaskar or Nala Najan.

The choreographer's overall composition: Every item of dance was certainly composed by someone. Whoever composed it was most certainly creative, whatever field of dance the work was in, including the ethnic forms. What is eternally wearying is the layman's attitude that a neoclassic composition is "just another Spanish dance." Surely La Argentinita's *Bolero* or Mariano Parra's *Romanza Gitana* are highly creative works. The problem is that the critic and audience are unaware of the knowledge and techniques upon which these works are built. The weakness, then, lies not in the performer and choreographer but in the watcher. It is extremely improbable that new approaches will be recognized unless the watcher becomes erudite in the traditional forms.

The pioneering of adaptations: Admitting that what was new ten years ago is not new today, let us nevertheless glance briefly at the past, for adaptations have always been recognized in both ballet and modern dance but seldom if ever in the ethnic forms. In this country the first adaptations in the ethnic concert field were introduced by Denishawn. For the ethnic-dance student, performer, or watcher who would fully appreciate the pioneering genius of Ruth St. Denis I recommend reading attentively the book by Ted Shawn titled *Ruth St. Denis: Pioneer and Prophet,* published in 1920. Miss St. Denis based her works on a profound study of the philosophies, histories, paintings, and sculptures of the Oriental lands. What she created was true, although traditional techniques were generally absent.

La Argentina pioneered an adaptation when she used Spanish classical music and danced to it with a new and subtle awareness of the musical phrase and mood. With this solo work she created a new school of Spanish dance, later called the neoclassic form, that in the hands of fine and knowledgeable choreographers grew into group works of exceptional value. Unfortunately, such works still go unrecognized by many as the highly creative works they truly are. Pioneering figures in this field are rising all about us. Let us hope they will meet with wider recognition than that accorded Maracci and Luisillo, for only through recognition at home can the pioneering ethnic choreographer of America build new bridges to wider horizons for our country's dance arts.

The creation of movements and motivations: As observed earlier in this chapter, any number of departures from the traditional have already been made, but the possibility of untried creative works remains a rich field. For the young choreographer interested in probing this facet of ethnic dance let me issue a word of warning.

The motivations for creative ethnic compositions should be only those that are common to all mankind. One of the identifying characteristics of ethnic dance is that it springs from an emotion common to all peoples, albeit the form of expression changes from folk to folk. That is why this form of dance speaks so strongly to the alien watcher. People are interested in basic and universal emotions, not personalized problems. The nine *rasas* (see chapter

39

ten) point the way to these basic emotions. If we express fear, let us express fear of the unknown—an emotion felt by all people in all ages—not our own little neuroses.

Several of the previously noted pioneers made their earliest departures in the use of authentic music. This has proven to be good theater, for the average audience is not conditioned to the sound of Oriental music (including, until very recently, flamenco) and often resents it to the point of staying away from the theater. However, for the choreographer it is not always an easy way. To use ethnic techniques with nonethnic music demands a sound knowledge of musicology. One must be aware not only of rhythm and melodic line but of accent, phrasing, and the emotional intention of the composer. The dancer must first learn to move to note values, then to rhythm, then to melodic scheme, and finally to the full gamut of musical dynamics—accelerando and ritardando, crescendo and diminuendo, staccato and legato—for the dynamics of kinetic emotional expression are typified in the dynamics of music. The dancer, like an instrument, must feel complete identification with the music, for music is the essence of movement. In the raising of the pianist's hands or the lifting of the violinist's bow we see the oppositional attack that so strengthens movement. And in music lies the key to the most difficult element of dance composition—the dramatic design—for music is built on just such a design.

If movement and music become one, then the watcher hears what he sees, and both those senses work together toward his emotional understanding. The goal of stage dance is communication with the audience, to reach the watcher and move him emotionally. All things relevant to the scope of the work must conspire to enchain the audience—the movements, motivation, music, costumes, lights, the building of the program itself. Dance is an ephemeral art that dies aborning. All that is left when the curtain falls is what the watcher remembers. Audience communication depends not on what work is danced but on how that work is danced. Always remember that art is capable of perfection, but the artist is not.

You cannot do creative work with one eye on the gallery. You cannot do creative work consciously following a prevailing trend. Above all, you cannot do creative work if the emotional content is outside your personal experience. Every movement, every gesture, every glance must be dredged up out of your personal emotions. One must know, and know at first hand, the personal physical reactions to great events, and even more, know the nearly infinitesimal details that start the soul on the endless search for the why of the universe and the ultimate realization of one's own place in its pattern. This is the subject matter for great creative works— the eternal question that plagues men of all climes and all ages. The soul searching of the individual has no valid message unless that searching is within the experience of all men. If you do not love and sympathize with all humanity, your message can reach only those few whom you do love and understand. Your creative work must touch the heartstrings of your watchers with the vibration of their own emotional experiences. So you must speak in a language that is at once universal in its basic message and abstract in its possibilities of inner interpretation. Create within your own experience and with an honest desire to touch with sympathy the hidden hearts of those who may watch you.

five

Swan Lake and Bach-Bharata

The creative possibilities inherent in Hindu *natya* are almost limit-less. In the winter of 1944 I closed my eyes and jumped off a precipice by staging *Swan Lake* (Act II), in Hindu dance idiom. I could not believe the stir this ballet caused in the dance field, and certainly I could never have guessed that twenty-five years later Matteo would restage this work with his Indo-American Company and that it would again cause something of a furor. Echoes were heard even in India, and *SPAN* magazine (November 1970) de-voted a story and a cover to Matteo's production.

Matteo was not in the original cast, but he partnered me in the re-creation of the work when it was staged by Edna Dieman's Theater of Two Worlds at Jacob's Pillow in 1964.

In my own theater we performed this ballet some three hun-dred times, the cast changing with my changing companies. We also went on the road with it in many cities in this country.

In 1946 I choreographed a work to music of Bach. This also was danced many times, although it never proved as popular as *Swan Lake,* which seems to be box office in whatever idiom. How-ever, the *Bach-Bharata* was restaged with Nala Najan as the soloist at Jacob's Pillow in the summer of 1971.

During the golden age of the forties it was my custom to add to my printed programs a mimeographed sheet that explained (or excused, if you will) the reasoning behind my somewhat unorthodox departures from tradition. The rest of this chapter consists of explanations accompanying the debuts of *Swan Lake* and *Bach-Bharata.*

Tchaikovsky's Swan Lake in the Idiom of the Indian Dance

In spite of my conviction that the balletomanes will tear me limb from limb, I have staged Tchaikovsky's *Swan Lake* following the general lines of Ivanov's choreography but in the orthodox technique of Hindu *natya.*

The idea came about in this way. Attending a performance of ballet by one of the several excellent companies now working in this country, I found one of the evening's features to be *Swan Lake.* Of course I had seen this ballet several times before, but on this occasion I was with one of my *natyas,* and we discussed at length (and with gestures) the inadequacy of the pantomime. As we talked about it during the intermission I quoted the drama critic John Anderson, who wrote, "Where I break down and go to the dunce's corner is when the dancers go through a lot of action and I find that for all the meaning I get out of it the corps de ballet might have been wrapped in burlap bags and left in the basement."

Well, one thing led to another. I mentioned my reactions to Anatole Chujoy one evening. He agreed with me and during the ensuing discussion told me a great deal about the pantomime of the western dance. (He has begun—and, we hope, will shortly finish—a book that deals with this subject.) He told me that the conventional pantomime of the classical ballet was invented by the protagonists of that art, and in inventing it they were guided by things of the same genre that had gone before them. For example, it is generally conceded that much of the pantomime came from the Italian commedia dell'arte. But Italy is probably not the origin of pantomime. Perhaps it came through Spain from the Moors (who, we assume, got it from India). This is Mr. Chujoy's feeling. Lincoln Kirstein writes that ancient Greece is the source of Italy's gestures. (But Greece may have gotten pantomime from the Orient.) Or perhaps (I offer) the gesture language grew up in southern Italy and Spain because of the Oriental mariners who passed that way. I know that many of the Andalusian and Neapolitan gestures are identical with the accepted classical *mudras* of Bharata. Mr. Chujoy pointed out to me a score of gestures that are identical in *natya* and ballet.

The ballet's conventional pantomime may have begun some three hundred years ago when ballet as a classical theater-dance form did. Certainly *La Fille Mal Gardée*, the first ballet (as we understand the term *ballet*), was produced nearly two hundred years ago and presented in the first and second acts long passages of conventional mimed dramatic action. Mr. Chujoy also observed that the pristine clarity of the ballet pantomime has largely been lost and mentioned several rather amusing incidents in which the sense of the story has been sacrificed completely to the acrobatic technique of the protagonists. Many scenes of pure pantomime have been cut completely, and in the one-act version, which we now generally see as *Swan Lake,* the libretto serves only as an invisible thread upon which are strung the pearls of pirouettes, *jetés,* and *batterie.*

Since this chance meeting with Mr. Chujoy, the conviction to stage Tchaikovsky's ballet in Hindu style has grown slowly but steadily in my mind. These are my several reasons for undertaking it: First, to show the great clairty of Hindu gestures when applied to a well-known story (which is, of course, inevitably the case in India, since all Indians know their own great epic tales). Second, to show that the technique of Hindu *natya* is so complete that the thrill of pirouettes and leaps need not be sacrificed. Without introducing one step or posture that has not been classified in the palm-leaf manuscripts of the past that deal with this complete art-science, one may follow the general lines of the ballet as laid down by Ivanov, display physical technique, and yet not lose the story itself. Mindful that someone may doubt the authenticity of some of these steps, I have written down the choreography with the Sanskrit technical terms. Any balletomane may check these terms against the steps they will have seen, while any complete student of the classical Hindu school will find this text clear to re-stage this ballet exactly as you will see it here. Third, there are those who feel that the Hindu dance is limited. I hope through this ballet to prove to many doubters that it is not. You will see that the range of technical virtuosity and style surpasses that of ballet. Furthermore, the Hindu technique need not always be applied to the stories of India's epics. Many of us know that today in India Shankar is applying the Hindu technique to *natyas* of modern social significance. There are many fairy tales of both East and West that might be staged in Hindu technique with rare beauty.

The original libretto of *Swan Lake* called for a production of four acts, which lasted three hours. It was first produced in Moscow in 1877, the choreography being by Julius Reisinger. A recent biography of Tchaikovsky by Weinstock states that the composer was dissatisfied with the production, and, indeed, when costumes and scenery wore out, the ballet was dropped from the repertoire. However, in 1894 (after the death of Tchaikovsky) *Swan Lake* was revived in full in St. Petersburg. The new choreography was by Marius Petipa (first and third acts) and Lev Ivanov (second and fourth acts), and new scenery and costumes graced the production.

Diaghilev presented a one-act version of *Swan Lake* (the second act), and the Ballet Russe de Monte Carlo does this version. Ballet Theatre does a newer version with choreography by Anton Dolin. A part of the third act is now being given by the Ballet Russe de Monte Carlo under the title *The Magic Swan.*

I am presenting the second act and a prologue. The prologue is a purely pantomimic scene between the Rakshasa (Sorcerer) and the girl who is transformed. It is, choreographically as well as musically, the introduction to the ballet. It would be impossible to tell a Hindu *natya* without some explanatory action to introduce the *nrtta* passages.

Ramachandran, the John Martin of the Deccan, attended all my recitals in Madras. In those recitals I covered quite a range of dance techniques, as those of you who know me can imagine. After seeing all my recitals and conferring often with me and my husband about music and dance theories and techniques, he wrote

46

that although the West could learn from the East as to the scientific approach to the dance art, the East could learn from the West anent the science of music. If Ramachandran was right, then perhaps our own conception of *Swan Lake* is an ideal marriage of East and West into a global theater dance.

I know that my own students, most of whom have never studied any dance technique but the eastern and its derivatives (always accompanied by original music), are worked into a state of trembling enthusiasm about the appropriateness of each movement to the music, and have already begun to feel that only this *karana* would be appropriate to that phrase of Tchaikovsky's composition.

Another interesting point I have discovered in making this *natya* ballet is the application of the mental science of Hindu dance. That is to say, I myself studied ballet some years (about ten altogether). In approaching this experiment, I was very much afraid that the sound of the music would bring out in me only *jetés, pirouettes,* and *relevés.* But *natya* stood me in good stead. I just emptied out the accumulated impressions of many years of study—thought Hindu, felt Hindu—and there it was.

Those of you who know me well know that my scope has been, is, and probably always will be the desire to serve the dance. I do not build to collect applause, press notices, or high salaries. I build something because I am convinced it is a good thing to do. I do think this is a good thing to do. For the Hindu dance it will prove to unbelievers the several points I have already mentioned. For the ballet it has this to offer: Ballet, like any art that is alive, is in evolution. It needs new material, new approaches, new angles. Ballet choreographers are aware of this, for they have already borrowed from the Spanish dance (*El Sombrero de Tres Picos, El Amor Brujo*) and the modern dance (*Choreartium, Three Virgins and a Devil, Pillar of Fire*). Attempts have also been made to borrow from the East, yet except in the case of the Near East, these ballets have not proven successful. *Le Dieu Bleu*—a story of Krishna choreographed by Fokine with Nijinsky in the title role—did not survive in spite of the combined efforts of these two geniuses. I am

47

convinced this ballet would be successful if it employed Hindu techniques to tell this very Hindu tale. A number of other purely Indian stories have been used by the ballet, with very relative success (*Sakuntala,* from Kalidasa's classic play, *Lalla Rookh* of Thomas Moore, etc.).

I am sure that the staging of *Swan Lake* in Indian dance idiom will cause quite a lot of discussion and that *natya*manes as well as balletomanes will find the idea something of a blasphemy. Already I am hearing objections on the grounds of my own unwavering authenticity. Because I have objected to Hindu ritual dances set to boogie-woogie, I am being accused of doing the same thing when I set Hindu technique to western music. Need I explain that my own choreography is scarcely the same as the age-old rituals of India and that Tchaikovsky and Cole Porter are not striving for the same emotional impact?

If we must have a simple thought from which to depart in order to organize the logic of this East-West experiment, I suggest that the watcher imagine that a Hindu gentleman, having just returned from an extended trip to Europe, is asked by his children and their friends to tell them a story (a very usual situation in India). So this gentleman takes out the records of *Swan Lake* and tells the story, illustrating it with Tchaikovsky's music (also the usual way of telling a tale in India—to illustrate it with music in the proper mood). What happens on our stage is that the Indian children visualize the tale as it unfolds. Just as the original German fairy tale could live only in a child's imagination, so this new visualization can live only in a child's imagination—this time, a Hindu child.

One gentleman, when told of *Swan Lake* in Hindu dance idiom, cried, "My God! How apalling!"

I see what he means; I would surely react in practically the same way if the Ballet Russe staged Shankar's *Shiva Parvati Nrttya Dwandva* to Shirali's music with their own dance technique. Yet I submit that the difference lies in the point that this is an experiment offered in a very modest and *intime* experimental theater. I,

48

(*Left to right*) Ruth St. Denis, Mei Lan Fang, and Ted Shawn. (Photographed in Peking, 1925)

(*Left to right*) Ted Shawn, Ruth St. Denis, La Meri, and Jose Limon at Jacob's Pillow, 1964. (Photo: John Van Lund)

Swan Lake (revival): Jacob's Pillow Festival, 1964. (*Left to right*) Matteo, La Meri, and the Dieman-Bennett Company. (Photo: John Van Lund)

Bach-Bharata Suite: Jacob's Pillow Festival, 1971. Nala Najan as soloist with the Ethnic Dance Arts Company. (Photo: John Van Lund)

Sahomi Tachibana (Japanese dancer par excellence).

Huayno (Peru) by the Ethnic Dance Arts Company, 1973. (Photo: Images)

Charles Moore as a Watusi warrior at the Ethnic Dance Arts Festival, 1972.

Jean-Léon Destiné, Haitian dancer.

even more than you, am convinced that there is no permanent wedding between pure Hindu technique and pure ballet libretto and choreography. But exaggerations must be done briefly in two directions before an artistic balance is reached, and I reiterate that there is something that each of these two dance arts can learn from the other. A fusion there can be. *El Amor Brujo* was as impossible of artistic realization by Pastora Imperio, *gitana pura,* as it is by a pure ballet company, yet both Mercé and La Argentinita, combining in themselves complete knowledge of both Spanish and ballet traditions, have staged it successfully.

As a whole the technical style used is that of the renaissance school of modern India (the school represented, if not actually created by, Shankar). But in certain numbers and in certain characters and moments the style is purer. The character of the Rakshasa is Kathakali. The second solo of Hamsa-rani is pure North Indian. The quartet of the little swans is in Bharata Natyam style. The bird movements of Hamsa-rani at her transformation, as well as in her first solo, are from Kathakali.

The program that provides the remainder of the evening's entertainment has been selected to prepare the audience by showing authentic examples of the source material. *Gauba's Journey to Paradise* is a Hindu fairy tale set to Hindu music and combines the North Indian dance technique with the more complete South Indian *hasta* vocabulary. Since the subject is gay rather than grave, it is believed that the pantomimic action is relatively easy to follow.

The seven classical dances that form the second part of the program present seven of the outstanding types of Indian dance styles—those styles from which the technical material for *Swan Lake* has been drawn.

The libretto and the accompanying music forced us to break two of Bharata's stage rules: that a death in the realistic sense (*lokadharma*) may not be presented on the stage and that evil may not finally triumph over good. For these freedoms we hope to be forgiven.

49

The Bach-Bharata Suite

In the winter of 1944 I made my first radical departure from pure authenticity in setting Hindu technique to Tchaikovsky's ballet of *Swan Lake.* In the years in which I had been building my experimental theater, founded with Ruth St. Denis in 1940, I had made quite a number of renaissance, but still authentic, ethnologic ballets—*Gauba's Journey, Krishna-Gopala, Devi Murti, Amor Brujo, Iberia,* and several less popular dance-dramas. But my first radical departure from the usual—the traditional combination of a classic-eastern tale interpreted by means of classic eastern technique, set to classic western music—was accomplished (not without some trepidation on my part) in Tchaikovsky's *Swan Lake* with the encouragement and guidance of that great aesthete and balletomane Anatole Chujoy. I confess the success of this venture exceeded my greatest hopes, and the performance attendance by great ballet exponents such as Romanoff, Hightower, Krassovska, Kaye, Svetlova, and others gave me real joy.

The following season (March 1945) I staged Rimsky-Korsakov's *Scheherazade,* using as libretto the tales selected by the composer instead of the story that Fokine set to the same music. This composition proved to be even better "theater" than the *Swan Lake,* which had first broken with tradition.

In January 1945 I presented for the first time a series of western hymns and spirituals interpreted with Hindu *hasta mudras.* Frankly, I considered them only an amusing little divertissement and was amazed at the controversies they aroused among *natya*-manes. However, the easeful joy of doing this type of thing and the endlessness of the field brought me to experiment more and more with the form. In the summer of 1945 I presented at Ted Shawn's University of the Dance, Jacob's Pillow, these gesture songs in collaboration with Sylvia Leicht, soprano. Success was immediate and wholehearted, and we have even successfully toured the South with these songs. A short while ago, in March 1946, I presented a whole program of gesture songs and drew forth the sincere accolade of a complete article by Walter Terry.

The *Bach-Bharata Suite* is another departure, such as *Swan Lake, Scheherazade, Gesture Songs,* yet it is entirely different from all three.

Swan Lake used traditional music, libretto and choreographic design, changing only the actual physical idiom from ballet to *natya.* It set out to prove the versatility and dramatic impact of Hindu pantomime.

Scheherazade used traditional music but eschewed both the libretto and choreographic design of the ballet. It set out to prove that a tale is best told in its own language.

The Indo-American *Gesture Songs* quite simply set traditional and classic eastern gestures to traditional and typical western songs. This form seems to prove that the emotional experience of people in both the East and the West is so identical that when both expressions are sincere and basic, they can be wedded with no violence done to either art.

In the *Bach-Bharata Suite* I have selected typical excerpts from the music of Johann Sebastian Bach and interpreted them in pure dance (*nrtta*), using the oldest known dance technique, the Bharata Natyam of South India. With this I hope to set forth three things: (1) that Bharata Natyam is a *style of movement* and, far from being a purely racial and ethnologic vehicle, can be used as a technique to interpret the abstract dance art of any nationality of artist. At the same time perhaps I shall prove to young students that this dance science can be used as a form of self-expression. The Hindu has written, "Even if you are not with us, we are with you." (2) I hope to remind westerners that the hand gesture is only a very characteristic fraction of the complete dance science of Bharata Natyam and that the body control includes floor contacts, extensions, elevations, turns, and all the movements of other dance arts heretofore considered more space-covering. (3) I hope to set forth the universality of the artist-creator by combining the architectonic technical expression of ecclesiastical inspiration of two widely separated sources, Bach (1685-1750) and Bharata (who in the third century put into manuscript notes the technique that had been building since the third millenium B.C.).

51

In March 1945 Dr. Henry Marx, reviewing *Scheherazade,* wrote, "Here music and dance are moulded into a perfect unity and one wishes that La Meri would sometime interpret Bach music in dance, for the Indian idiom seems peculiarly suited for it." To Dr. Marx, then, goes first credit for this suite. Credit for the first choreographic step made in this medium goes to Juana, who in the fall of 1944 interpreted *Bach-Karanas* by means of archaic Bharata Natyam.

The *Bach-Bharata Suite* is another step forward in a medium that may prove almost endless in possibilities—massed chorales, dance accompaniment of great symphony orchestras—for this friezelike architectonic movement lends itself admirably to the biggest halls and stadiums. No one in the United States could know better than I how often producers and managers have refused Hindu dance technique on the grounds of its delicacy being unsuited to the enormity of American auditoriums. Here, surely, is their answer.

The pages of Bach have been chosen as samples of the various ways in which the art expressions of Bach and Bharata can be combined.

The Art of the Fugue (First Movement)

Following the lead of the composer, I have taken the four thematic bars, conceived them as a physical design of (1) side, (2) side, (3) oblique, (4) circular, and on this simple base worked out a variety of floor, air, and body designs.

Two-Part Inventions

The inventions are visualized by Lillian Rollo (treble) and Juana (bass). In the first invention the various musical phrases are each interpreted with a corresponding *karana* (full combination), these *karanas* recurring in the bass and treble as the music wills. The sixth invention is done solely by means of *thatadavu* (floor contacts), again the dance patterns following the music design.

Air on the G String

This solo (La Meri) uses a simple formula in which the dancer's upper body follows the melodic line while the lower body follows the accompaniment. Since the music itself contains a strong emotional color, the dance, too, must project an abstract emotionalism.

"Come, Sweet Death"

Here the chorale form is used, the dancers employing only the upper body to visualize the words sung and emotions projected.

Concerto in D Minor (Allegro)

As a finale to the suite the dancers move in a freer floor design, utilizing some of the more dynamic techniques of Bharata Natyam (*alaga, krpalaga, akasa, bhramari, udvrtta, anga,* and so on). The soloist (La Meri) interprets the solo piano while the four other dancers (Juana, Lillian Rollo, Edna Dieman, Rebecca Harris) move for the orchestra. It will easily be seen that choreographic design repeats with repetition of musical design. Indeed, the whole choreographic theory is as simple as the basic melodies upon which Bach has based his compositions. Yet is not simplicity the most convincing of proofs?

In the hope that some young dancer-choreographer will follow the signpost set up by Walter Terry, I include cuttings from an article written by him and published in the *New York Herald-Tribune* on April 7, 1946. If it is read carefully, it will be seen that Mr. Terry points out three different roads to a career that can be taken by one who will prepare himself with a comprehensive study of Indian *hasta mudras.*

A dance event of historical significance and one that will unquestionably influence dance art and dance entertainment of the future occurred a few days ago in a little theater that in the past housed two great dance revolutionaries, Isadora Duncan and Ruth St. Denis. A few seasons ago the Texan La Meri transformed this famous studio into a miniature theater and here she has given weekly performances of her ethnologic dances from many lands. Respected as a scholar, interpreter and performer, La Meri has drawn to her theater persons who are eager to learn about the dances of other peoples rather than those who are primarily pleasure seekers, but her new dance discovery promises to be universal in its appeal, for it opens up a new avenue to dance creation and it embodies in it the ingredients of highly sophisticated entertainment. . . .

Immediately apparent is the fact that a vast literature of song, both sacred and secular, is available for gesture-song treatment. The selection of choral works would make possible the development of this idiom to include group gesture-dance, and I can assure you that La Meri's beautiful, reverent and stirring interpretations of hymns and spirituals almost cry out for inclusion in appropriate church services. In the field of smart entertainment, gesture-dances to popular songs constitute a novelty that might easily develop into a permanent amusement attraction. It is not beyond the realm of possibility that ballet could adapt portions of this gesture language to spruce up the now weak and obscure traditional mime; in fact, any highly stylized form of theater could find much of merit and usability in this gesture technique.

six

Ethnic Dance Appreciation

In the beginning the dance was life. In primitive man dancing was absolute and the ritual of religion. Inarticulate, he, like the waves of the mighty sea, praised his god in rhythm. So dance was born as the highest of the arts and was nurtured as the most respected of man's expressions.

The scope of art is higher and deeper than that of mere entertainment. Today it is the scope of the dance art to give to its audiences two hours of entertainment, of joy, yet also to send them away the richer through knowledge gained and through a new beauty seen and understood. Perhaps it is more difficult of apprehension than music or poetry, for it depicts the most spiritual of ideals through the most positive of vehicles.

The audience is half the performance of the art, for without the fine-tuned receiving set the melody, no matter how perfect, is lost in the void. The receiving set of judgment must be attuned to the length of the waves, or the static of imperfect knowledge coarsens and spoils all. Beauty is the exclusive property of the one who experiences it. Yet to see beauty one must clear one's mind of the weeds of false opinions. Let us not take our opinions ready-made from others. Let us not believe that because a familiar art is a beautiful one, the beautiful art can only be a familiar one. If we cannot see beauty, let us not declare it nonexistent, but let us have the courage to admit that as yet we are blind to it.

To the born aesthete, unafraid of public opinion, beauty, however alien, speaks clearly and directly. But these are rare persons. Many who hunger for the impact of a strange beauty cannot see without the mitigating bifocals of a little understanding of the ideals inherent in an alien art. In the last analysis the watcher's desire for a knowledge of the techniques of an art form springs from the necessity to get his consciousness of ignorance out of his way so he can allow his aesthetic emotions to function without hindrance.

Critic and public know and judge ballet and modern dancers on their own merits. This is not yet true for the ethnic dancer. A norm of judgment has not yet been learned, and the dancer too often suffers from the watchers' lack of understanding of both techniques and motivations. The traditional and authentic are confused in the mind of the watcher, and thus the creative work of the artist goes unrecognized. Departures and neoclassic works are often frowned upon because the watcher has only just learned to appreciate the traditional and so excludes all else. But our field is not a static one. The techniques we learn can be, are, and must be employed for contemporary and personal expression.

Watchers of ethnic dance forms are often bewildered by the glamorous costumes and strange techniques and seldom look beneath these superficialities to feel the emotional depths of these expressions or even analyze the kinetic and dynamic qualities that are the essence of their being. Look behind the costume, for the dance is not all costume. I have become so aware of this that I have often done lecture-demonstrations in rehearsal dress and have invariably found that audience reaction was amazement at the difference in body techniques. But in many cases the costume itself is made to dance, and this is again a difficult technique. When they are handled by an artist, there is striking beauty in the architectonic sleeves of a Japanese kimono, in the sensuous and rhythmic lift of the Spanish *bata* (trailed dress), in the staccato fling of the Javanese *sampour* (scarf).

The Japanese say that "art is hidden by its own perfection." This is the ideal of the ethnic dancer—to make it all look easy.

And (once you have looked beyond the costume) it gives the
watcher the impression that just anyone can do it! Sometimes
the student's awakening after a few months of study can be very
rude indeed! For it is not all that easy! It is the very perfection
of the art that hides the difficulty of the technique.

Few indeed are the foreigners capable of judging ethnic dance
arts beyond the point of an instinctive aesthetic reaction to great
beauty. And because in many forms of ethnic dance the art carries
the artist, the strangeness and strength of the art itself is believed
to be the strength of the artist.

Inversely, once the strangeness has worn off, the watcher (or
critic) reaches that no man's land between instinctive reaction and
knowledgeable judgment and is quite incapable of seeing the inner
qualities of the individual artist. By inner qualities I mean the
good points—expressive hands, controlled toes, sincere emotionalism—that might momentarily be overshadowed by drawbacks
such as youth, inexpertness, or even present difficulties—a bad
stage or poorly played music. The knife cuts two ways. A watcher,
accustomed all his life to ballet, applauds vigorously the "technique" of a young ethnic dancer although that dancer locks his
knees, which in this field is a technical error as grave as loose knees
in ballet. But we are accustomed to certain lines and we loudly
condemn all others. We have not yet learned (with the Javanese)
that the cultured person is possessed of humility and lowers his
eyes, that only the vulgar go through life with wide, staring eyes
and open mouth.

The ethnic dance is the product of the necessity for pure
emotional expression. Even the casual observer will concede this
point to the Spanish dance. Purely emotional, from egotistic castanets to sadistic heels, and sexually aware in every line of both
masculine and feminine bodies, it has no reason to exist at all without the driving strength of emotional expression behind it. But
the Javanese dance is not less the product of the necessity for
emotional expression. Here again we must not think the emotional level of all people is identical with our own. We, like the Spaniard, must "spit it out," "get it off the chest." But the easterner

must rise above, must seek Brahmananda. Can you watch the Javanese dance without feeling a strange, new calm envelope you? This is choreography with an unequaled power, for it carries a quasi hypnotism in which watcher and dancer seem to leave themselves behind and lift their astral bodies to move in some suspended place between heaven and earth. But we are afraid of this hypnotism; we squeeze our eyes shut like frightened children and whine, "I don't like it! It isn't exciting!" It is exciting, but on a far higher plane. Our fear has made us intolerant and unfriendly, not only toward exotic dances but toward each other. Indeed, the unfriendliness and intolerance of the individual dancers toward each other is a heavy deterrent in the development of America's dance. The strange, snobbish scorn for those who "are not as I am" is an evil factor in the dance world, already struggling under the too-heavy burden of the technical unions and managerial trusts. Even within a given field of dance, the open antagonism among dancers is a strange and sore point. Why, why should an artist feel that by disparaging another artist he promotes himself? Nothing could be further from the truth. To the thoughtful listener his meanness is so apparent that one knows immediately he lacks the greatness of soul that is the outstanding attribute of the true artist. To quote an eminent ethnic dancer: "The artist does this cruel thing to his fellow artist. They lacerate each other . . . each one in turn tears down the other . . . guru to guru and dancer to dancer." Such pettiness closes forever the doors to true artistry, which comes only through tolerance and deep understanding.

Ethnic dancers specializing in one style only are called Spanish dancers, Hindu dancers, or at most Oriental dancers; but my own talent has lain not in the further perfection of a single form but in breadth of interpretation of the bodies, techniques, psychologies and souls of the many peoples of East and West alike. This type of study engenders a great tolerance, which is often mistaken for lack of dedication, while technical ease and a deep personal love for the peoples represented give to the uninitiated the impression that the dancer is "tossing it off." This is a grave error brought about by western habits of thinking. We have come to consider the word *technique* applicable only to movements that are so showy as to approach acrobatics—leaps, turns, extensions. The term actually applies also to the arms, hands, head, dynamics, and emotional expression in any type of dance, and it is an error to applaud a dancer if his leaps are high but his shoulders and fingers tensed. The aficionado of the Spanish dance seldom employs the word *technique.* It is too all-embracing to be used casually. He says that La Argentina's castanets are without equal, that Pastora Imperio's *brazeo* (arm carriage) is divine. And he is fully aware that technique is useless unless it is put at the service of emotionalism.

In the Oriental dance the whole focus of attention changes. The technical vehicle of expression is the upper body, culminating in the hands and face. The lower body is the rhythmic accompaniment to the melody of the upper body. But rare indeed is the westerner who can refocus his attention to watch the eastern dance. The *punkhita* hand, like the Spanish castanets, does not look difficult, so its mastery evokes no applause, either manual or printed, such as accompanies the execution of the thirty-two *fouettés.* Let me parenthesize here and now that the great ballerinas are not deluded by ease of execution into believing the exotic techniques are easy! As all the dance world must know by now, many years ago Uday Shankar choreographed an Indian ballet for the immortal Anna Pavlova. He has told me that at every performance she wept copiously because of her inadequate Indian technique. This matchless ballet artist always had a great emotional craving for ethnic dance, as a study of her life will show. She worked with Spanish, Indian, Japanese, and Mexican dance, although after much study she considered herself inadequate for the performance of some of these forms.

Certain general facts apply to all dances of the Orient. It is well to keep these in mind, since the Occidental dance differs in nearly all these points.

1. All eastern dance was born of worship; all has a legendary beginning related to God (in whatever form He took for the worshipers). This may be why the eastern dance puts the burden of

performance on the upper body, for Delsarte has shown us that the most spiritual expression is in this area (see chapter eight).

2. The emotional choreographic structure is built not to amaze or amuse but to soothe and uplift . . . perhaps even to induce a state of trance.

3. The weight of centuries is behind the traditions of techniques, costumes, and makeup, and all these accept change slowly if at all.

4. There is a marked difference in masculine and feminine technique. A woman should "sway like a willow"; a man should "jump like a tiger."

5. Drama and dance are one. It is inconceivable that one can dance without acting or act without movement.

6. In dance-dramas good always triumphs. (It is not the West that invented psychological dramas, as even a cursory look at the plots of ancient Chinese dramas will show.)

7. India has had a strong influence throughout the East. In many lands the themes of dance-dramas are taken from India's epics and stories of Saivite interest.

8. Rulers interested themselves deeply in dance-dramas— supported them, performed them, and made them a part of general education. Where the court's influence was long we find the heroic figure always of great gentility.

9. In nearly all cases these dances were born of and for the folk and are forever an integral part of their lives. Thus the dances have survived many centuries of wars, pestilence, and death. Everyone in the audience knows the story told and the way of its telling. It is a racial and national heritage. It is ethnic dance.

Let us take a brief look at the history of ethnic dance in the United States.

Ruth St. Denis and Ted Shawn, those two great figures to whom the dance arts of the United States owe so much, first gave the ethnic dance arts to our country. It is true they were preceded by exotic visitors—Lola Montez, Carmencita, and others—but these only opened a door through which we looked eagerly but briefly on an art that was not ours. The Denishawn Company was our own flesh and blood, and what they went away to find and bring back to America became our heritage. In these latter days their work is often called romantic, but actually it is, and was, of a substance a good deal more solid than the term *romantic* implies. For these two were in themselves an extraordinary combination. Mr. Shawn's approach to ethnic work was that of the serious student. Some of his presentations, such as *Momji Gari,* were utterly traditional; others were rearrangements of authentic techniques, such as the Japanese spear dance.

Miss St. Denis's approach was that of the poet, for she walked straight through tradition and authenticity of movement patterns to grasp the essential motivating spirit and linear design of the dance.

What better introduction could we have had to the dance arts of alien peoples? That the majority of Denishawn pupils followed another movement is part of the history of American modern dance. But there were some who followed ethnic ways, and these, with the two ever-active leaders, prepared American audiences for the appreciation of exotic dance forms and gave us our first lesson in the great truth that an art alien to our bodies need not be alien to our minds and hearts.

Post-Denishawn exponents of ethnic dance in the United States found a sympathetic audience awaiting them. In the Oriental field the late twenties and early thirties brought us Roshanara, Vera Mirova, Michio Ito; in the Spanish field, Escudero and La Argentina. A decade later Mei Lan Fang, Uday Shankar, and La Argentinita were names to conjure with. Some Americans, too, built their careers on the solid foundation of ethnic forms: Doris Niles, Carola Goya, Arthur Mahoney. During the forties the roster of top-flight artists grew to match the growing demand of the public: Carmen Amaya, Rosario and Antonio, Federico Rey and Pilar Gomez, Teiko Ito, Devi Dja, Mara, Hadassah, Asadata Dafora, Pearl Primus, Katherine Dunham, Jean-Léon Destiné, Tachibana, and many others.

This list of resounding names brings me to a repetition of the point that one need not be a native of the country that produced the dance form in order to perform it. Simkie, partner of Shankar, was a Parisian, yet she enchanted audiences all over the world, India not excluded. José Greco and Nila Amparo, two kids from Brooklyn, came home from touring Spain to conquer America. Reginald Laubin, finest exponent of Amerind dances twenty years ago, is American of Swedish stock. Ragini Devi, long an admired dancer of India and mother of Indrani, was born in Chicago. Federico Rey, partner to Argentinita, is Dutch. American-born are Sahomi Tachibana, Shrimathi Gina, Nala Najan, Matteo, Maria Alba, Mariano Parra, and many others. Indeed, the list of ethnic dancers contains as many foreigners as natives.

It is quite possible that if you are a lucky traveler, you will on very rare occasions see the best performance of an art in its native country. But it is sine qua non that you will also see the worst performance of that art in that same country. Antonio once told me that all the great forward movements in Spanish dancing came from outside Spain. This truth may be applied to many other forms of ethnic dance. In the past both Uday Shankar and La Argentina lived long abroad before they realized the full scope of their art.

One answer to the success of the foreigner is *work*. Americans (and English) are by nature hard workers. Latins and Orientals too often are not. By now we all know that talent is a drug on the market (and often the despair of teachers!) and that work is what makes success in art. You remember the quote often attributed to Fritz Kreisler: "Art is one tenth inspiration and nine tenths perspiration." So it is possible for the foreigner to beat the native at his own game. It won't be easy, but what worth having is? To quote John Martin: "I tell you this to show you that through devoted and untiring work you can make for yourself a place where none previously existed."

The teaching of ethnic dance, if properly done, requires a good deal more from teacher and pupils alike than might be supposed. In India the guru is said to have far more influence than the parents on the growth and formation of the pupil's character. For the study of the dance of the East entails not only the mastery of the physical techniques but spiritual and psychological growth. Without a knowledge and understanding of the culture, religion, and folkways that gave birth to the art, it is impossible to perform that art. This is equally true of Spain, Polynesia, and other Occidental lands. If both guru and pupil are native, backgrounds and social habits are relatively identical, and there is no need to begin by building a bridge of understanding. If the guru is native and the pupil foreign, then the latter must have great knowledge, great instinct, or both to ferret out and analyze the essential bodily, spiritual, and psychological differences between his own culture and that of his teacher. If both guru and pupil are foreign to the art with which they work, then the guru must carefully and individually resolve a system of disclosing to the pupil, step by step, the thousand subtle differences in the emanation and physical reactions of the native and the foreigner. If the pupil is young and open-minded and brings to his study a great love, a great desire, and an unquestioning respect, the way is possible. But the pitfalls are many, and to the guru each pupil presents a different psychological problem.

Ethnic dance was consolidated into that term during the golden age of dance in the United States. From the late twenties into the early fifties all types of dance flourished. The great creative moderns—Martha Graham, Doris Humphrey, Charles Weidman, José Limón, Helen Tamiris, and many others—were pioneering new forms of movement. The ballet companies were growing and coming from abroad—the New York City Ballet, the "baby ballerinas" of the Monte Carlo—and creative choreography (Antony Tudor, Jerome Robbins) was often presented. No less active was the ethnic field. Uday Shankar electrified the world; La Argentina and Argentinita enchanted audiences everywhere. Los Chavallilos, Escudero, Katherine Dunham, Pearl Primus, and many others were ever active, working creatively in their media.

But the halcyon days are past, and it would seem that we have returned to the superficialities of the early 1900s; "espanolismo" is rampant. Boleros are performed without castanets; whole programs are devoted entirely to flamenco, forgetting the rich heritage

63

of the folk and classical dance; the East Indian dancer has gone so "scholarly" that concerts become classroom exercises. And when dancers of other than ethnic schools touch on the ethnic, the means used are so superficial that they are laughable. Carmelita Maracci, that extraordinary choreographic genius, has written cuttingly on this situation in the book *The Dance Has Many Faces,* collected and edited by Walter Sorell. Her quarrel, like mine, is not that the ballet and modern dance use ethnic themes, but that the choreographer handles the techniques without taking the trouble to learn them. The essence of a racial dance can be felt and projected only through a knowledge of the physical vocabulary of that dance. Through conviction and the Other Thought comes quality, and quality is forever new. Acrobatics pall, and vague emoting bores.

True to our surroundings, Americans move big. We need to learn understatement of expression, and this we can learn from the Japanese. Sinda Iberia once said to an aspiring young dancer, "Keep moving! Only a true artist can afford to stand still!" Yet any six-year-old Japanese dancer can stand quite still and be expressive.

The true and dedicated artist respects his art, not his wonderful self. He does not follow the popular trends but his own convictions and knows himself to be a servant of dance, not a thief or a plagiarist in the infinite storehouse of the dance art. He does not use art for self-glorification or run gasping after a quick success. Although he may go to his grave with scarcely two pennies to lay on his closed eyes, he has been true to himself and to his dedication.

If the protagonist and audience could put aside our American habit of being in such a mad rush to get everything done yesterday, there is great joy to be found in the gentle walk down the unknown paths of ancient forests. Believe me, there is more beauty to be found while walking than while driving. Nothing worth having is acquired quickly. Learning to appreciate fully that subtle concordance of peoples, the ethnic dance, takes many years. No art is easy to learn, not even the art of living.

seven

The Spine

The teaching of ethnic dance forms by routines, as is often done in the land of origin, is entirely impractical when dealing with aliens. Exercises for body techniques are essential if one would turn a Brooklynite into a Hindu or an Iowan into a Spaniard.

Of course perfect ethnic characterization by an alien can sometimes be the product of a faultless instinct, which is due to a rare combination of mental and physical attributes. This happy situation is too rare to be counted on by the average student of ethnic techniques, still less by the average teacher of same.

Of first importance is the placement and control of the spine and its adjuncts—the neck, the shoulders, and the pelvis. I am aware that the control of the spine is necessary in all types of physical activity—modern dance, ballet, acrobatics, balancing, swimming, riding, even housework (unless you want to end up with your bosoms on your waist, your belly protruding and a permanent ache in your lower back). But we are herein concerned with the spine as a means of ethnic-dance characterization.

In many cases the dance techniques of two different peoples will differ more in the spine carriage than in any other part of the anatomy. Fast, loud *taconeo* is not the essence of flamenco, nor are soft, speaking hands the essence of Hawaiian dance. Consider the body carriage of the true Spanish dancer as compared to that of the average American woman!

65

The average American woman stands and walks with shoulders drooping forward, head outthrust, and pelvis slumped or, worse yet, relaxed backward with the whole weight of the upper torso sinking into the sacroiliac region. In short, we slump into our spines. (Is too much of our time spent with back relaxed into easy chairs and auto seats?) Men, too, slump into their spines and at thirty have undeveloped shoulders and the paunch of a man of sixty. Regard, by contrast, the Spanish dancer, with the chest springing upward, the spine straight, and the limbs moving easily from a controlled torso.

Let us examine in various peoples spine line, neck carriage, shoulders and pelvis.

At first glance it would seem that the spine line of the Chinese and Japanese female dancer is identical. Yet upon closer observation it will be seen that while the Chinese has a straight, free spine, the Japanese has a very slight forward curve in the upper spine and an under pull in the pelvic region. (For a westerner with an obtrusive derriere, this pull forward of the pelvis must be accentuated.) The Far Eastern woman is excessively feminine and modest, thus there is no pelvic movement in the dance. Shoulders are used only in moments of emotional stress. But the neck is both subtle and prevalent in both China and Japan.

There is no movement lovelier than the light lift of the chin and the soft droop to the shoulder in the Japanese dance. The neck, like a flower stem, seems weighted by the elaborate coiffure. It is written that the head of Chinese *tan* (female) is never still but moves always slightly, delicately, setting the wired spangles of her headdress aquiver.

As in all ethnic dance forms, masculine and feminine techniques must be considered separately. In both China and Japan the masculine spine line is straight; there are no pelvic movements, and shoulder and neck movements are strong and sharp.

The devadasi of South India is the protagonist of an art with several thousand years of development behind it (see chapter ten). In this dance form every possible movement of the body is controlled and carries emotional meaning. The spine in Bharata Natyam is plumb-line straight, and from this line the shoulders and neck are completely controlled and choreographed into the dance, leaving nothing to chance or the protagonist's temperament. In the ancient manuscripts setting forth the techniques of South Indian dance there is included a circular movement in the pelvis, a technique that has long been lost, perhaps during the "invasion" of Christianity. Characteristic of Orissi dance is the S curve of the spine—the side-thrust hip over a gentle leveling of the shoulders in opposition. This is a line often seen in Indian iconography. It is difficult to do correctly and can be achieved only by departing from a straight and erect spine with a shifting of the entire rib cage.

The Ceylonese and the Kathakali dancers have a unique spine line. Both are masculine; both very strong. The chest is upthrust, the back curved inward at the waist—a position that demands great suppleness and much practice.

In the north of India, where the dance takes a far different style, the spine is again tall and straight. The masculine dancer employs little or no shoulder and neck movements in rhythmic passages, but the female dancer will use both shoulders and neck and add a soft roll of the hip, all for rhythmic stress. Perhaps this usage is due to the Muslim influence in this part of the subcontinent.

Certainly the Muslim dances of the Near East are rich with shoulder and pelvic movements as well as the horizontal neck movements (*sundari*) of India, which have so caught the fancy of the Occidental. (I have seen an Arabic dancer with carefully trimmed spade beard swing his jaw from side to side in light-hearted imitation of the *sundari.*)

Surely everyone knows of the feminine Arabic dance presently called belly dance. This is a relatively recent development, stemming from an ancient ritual performed only in the chamber of a woman in childbirth. It was a means of assisting in the birth by the rhythmic contraction of the belly muscles. In ancient days men were not allowed to see this ritual. The nightclub belly dance is an offshoot, but in its present form even the techniques have

67

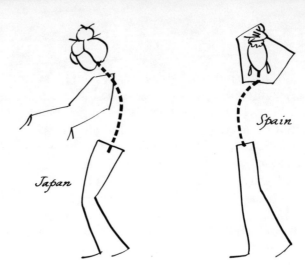

Japan

Spain

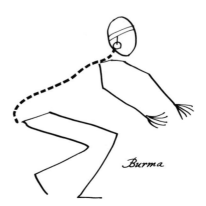

Burma

East Indian

Orissi

Kathakali

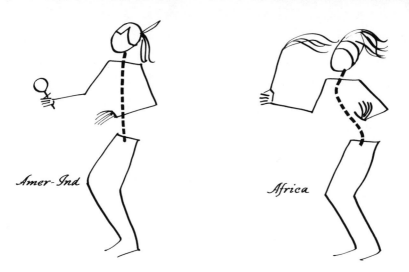

Amer-Ind

Africa

Bharata Natyam

Java

Bali

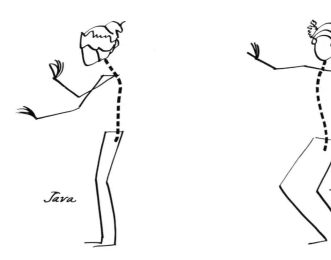

changed. Originally the pelvis was moved by the contraction in the belly muscles, and as late as 1930 the authentic belly dancer developed a very large belly from constant muscular work. In the version we see today the movement is controlled from the pelvis, much as in the Hawaiian hula, although there is a sharp contrast in the "strike" (Arabic) and "give" (Hawaiian) controls.

The Burmese "posture girl" has a most unique spine line. Leaning forward from the hips until the spine is nearly horizontal to the floor, she thrusts her neck upward. The onlooker seems to be viewing a head set on legs. The reason for this is hard to trace. It is known that in pre-Buddhistic days when the thirty-seven *nats* were Burma's bucolic gods formal dancing was done exclusively by priestesses. In all the Orient only in Burma have women, since time immemorial, held a position of equality with men. But the Burmese man does not bend his spine forward, although he, as well as his partner, has an extremely pliable waist and bends in any direction so low as to touch the floor.

In Java the origin of the *wayang wong* is the puppet play. Probably for this reason the spine is rigidly straight with the very slightest of tilts forward at the base, which gives all forward movement an effect of surging strength. Neck movements (*rourou* and *patakgulu*) are "floated" with great control. Pelvic movements are not used and the shoulders only in dramatic moments of great emotional stress. The neck and shoulder techniques are of Indian origin.

By contrast on Java's neighboring island, Bali, the spine is curved much as the Kathakali dancer's. Although there is no pelvic work, headdresses dance with quick neck movements, and shoulders are both expressive and decorative.

Let us briefly regard some of the Occidental ethnic dance forms. First, the Spanish dance, for here the body carriage is most obvious in its importance. Surely even the casual observer will see immediately the proud bearing of back and head and note the disastrous effect of its absence in a dancer of that style. Spain is very old in dance culture, and the south has been influenced greatly by the Caliphates (see chapter nine). In Andalusia the female spine line curves inward at the shoulder blades, forcing the chest out and up. Above this the spine pulls the head up and somewhat back from the last cervical vertebra and never loses this proud line. The dancer does *not* let the pelvic area swing backward to balance this upcurved chest, for the whole body drives upward. The masculine body line is much the same, save that the upper-spine curve becomes a straight line, and the pelvic region is held hard under in line with the proud head. (The torero could hardly leave his derriere protruding during a *media-veronica* lest the bull take undue advantage!) In Andalusia, as in the East, masculine and feminine techniques are quite different. In the flamenco the woman uses her shoulders rhythmically and as emotional effect; the man, seldom and very slightly. The woman may also use the pelvic area occasionally, but purists deplore this in the male dancer. The body carriage is more obviously important in Spanish dance than in any other western choreographic manifestation, and its acquisition is of first importance to the student of that dance form.

In South and Central America three different races have marked the dance style: Indian, African, and Spanish. The origin of any given dance can be recognized by the back line. In the *huayno* of the Inca Indians the spine is straight but with a very slight tilt forward, due to the locale (the high Andes) and the custom of carrying burdens on the back held by a broad band around the forehead. By contrast the *marinera,* danced in the cities of Peru, is Spanish in origin. The back line, while not so accentuated as the Spanish, is driven upward. In Brazil the dances show their African origins in many cases, although in the far interior they are purely Indian. Mexican dances in outlying districts are also purely Indian, while those of large cities show Spanish influence. It is an interesting study, and taken locale by locale, it will be found to hold true. (Indians in the Chaco or Paraguay use music and dance titles purely Spanish—*malagueña, zapateado*—but their dances as such are pure Indian.)

In many African tribes the pliability of the spine is almost unbelievable. Once seen, never forgotten are the spine, shoulders, and neck of the Watusi warrior. This amazing spinal succession shows again in certain dances of the Caribbean and Brazil. But in the north of the Dark Continent, where the Arabic influence is so strong, the spine succession is not used, and controlled shoulders and rhythmic necks become more apparent than the spine itself.

The Polynesians are the most sexually natural of all peoples. Within this race the spine carriage is an easy, natural uprightness, which is typical of those living with nature for many centuries. That these people use their hips is surely widely known—the easy, floating grace of Hawaiian dance and the lightening-quick semi-circular hip movement of the Tahitian. What is not so widely known is that in ancient days the female Hawaiian danced sitting down and also that the first grass skirts were brought to Hawaii from Tahiti by the missionary ship *The Morning Star.* The swinging hula skirt is only a graceful accompaniment to the speaking hands and has no emotional meaning in itself. It is interesting to note that in the days before the Caucasians went to the Islands, Hawaii had lying-down hulas designed to help childbirth, and these hulas were based on belly control much like that of the original belly dance of northern Africa. The Maoris also have such a belly dance—a physical exercise designed for therapy and performed by the entire population every morning on the village square. I have seen the older Maori women perform this as a dance amid gales of laughter from the native watchers.

We must not leave our discussion of the pelvic movements without a brief look at the Occidental distorted viewpoint of these techniques. We take the stand that pelvic movment is, per se, a sexual excitement. That such movements are not used in the highly stylized techniques of the Orient is not due to the lack of sex drive in the peoples themselves, but because the dance has a far more mystic function and is based on intellectual and emotional appeals. We tend to localize our notions about sex. Not so other peoples. To the Arabian the hair is very "sexy," and dances are performed that show off the dancer's long black hair through command of the neck and head. Indeed, we give to sex a good deal more importance than is its due. It is a very important part of life, but it is not uniquely responsible for every psychological ill. I have seen more ill humor from an empty stomach, more sorrow from an empty heart, and more bad art from an empty head.

In my many years of teaching ethnic dance art forms, I have found the student far too casual in his approach to the fundamental technique of the spine. It is my sincere conviction that without the control of the spine all mastery of the technique of the limbs is without flavor. The very lift of a leg changes character completely by the placement of the lower spine. The spine is the emotional thermometer. In proof we have only to observe the lifting back of "hope" and the drooping spine of "despair." The spine line shows not only immediate moods but also the mood character of a race—the pride of Spain, the natural joy of Polynesia, the dignity of the American Indian, the spiritual strength of India. Do not depend on your costume to identify your ethnic dance. You should be able to stand quite still in rehearsal leotard or jeans and set your spine in the proper line to attain immediate identification. (Can you imagine anything more ridiculous than an obi resting on the ledge of a protruding derriere?) Do not cozen yourself with the notion that you can, without training or control, just "feel it." Too many budding young dancers are convinced that they alone have "something to say" and all but the last soupçon to say it with. I can assure you that much of your Spanish *sangre* lies in your upper spine—the same place that harbors your Hindu "otherworldliness." You will have to do an inordinate amount of "feeling" before you can "feel it" above a sloppy and improper spine. The ballet gathers its strength from the torso. The modern dance sends its emotional impact from the same source. If your spine is not properly set for your ethnic techniques, you can express neither strength nor emotional impact. If you are dazzled by the fast turn and the high leap, realize that even these are the result of a controlled torso.

There are just so many directions in which a leg or an arm can be lifted. It is the *way* in which they are lifted that gives a lift character. And what lefts them? The muscles at the base where the limb joins the torso; the emotive quality behind the lift, which lies in the torso; the brain and heart behind the emotive quality, which gives life to the lift. These, too, lie in the torso.

So each dance style presents a different spine line and adjuncts control. It is futile to move the limbs in a given style if they move from an untrue torso. The very essence of style lies in the torso, and its control is a primal must for the dancer. Make your torso right and half your battle is won.

One of the greatest difficulties is to convince the student of the true importance of spine and adjuncts control. It is not enough to carry the torso correctly only during the hours of classes. It must be done all one's waking hours. The teacher cannot control your muscles. Only you can control them. A properly held spine must become as natural as breathing. It will affect not only your dancing but all your human contacts. No one disregards a person with a proud, free carriage. No one respects one with a craven, apologetic spine. Furthermore, all one's vital organs are affected adversely by a sodden spine. Could it be that this is the reason dedicated dancers stay young and healthy long after desk workers have accepted old age? Even if you never become a dancer, isn't it well worth a try?

eight

Exoteric and Esoteric Origins

In examining the movements and postures that characterize given ethnic dance arts we must look into the mores of the people who perform them, for their dance art is a sublimation of their everyday lives.

The characteristic posture and movements of each ethnic dance art are conditioned by

1. The clothes and foot covering
2. The place where danced
   a. Material (earth or floor)
   b. Spiritual (temple, palace, or theater)
3. Social customs
4. Religious beliefs
5. Earliest known origin of art
6. Physical conformation of the race

I call this the six-point source plan of exoteric origins, and this, together with the three-point plan (explained later in this chapter), is the guide, the yardstick, by which the student can measure ethnic-dance characterization and the teacher can bring to perfect flower the rare and little-understood talent of the natural artist.

We are now ready to consider some of the hundreds of examples that may serve as a beginning in the application of the six-point plan.

In about 894 A.D. Japan, which prior to that time had been dependent on China for costumes and customs, began to cultivate and perfect a culture of its own. It is from this point onward that we may consider the application of our plan. The garments of the women were both beautiful and enshrouding. At court a lady in her twelvefold robe might be wearing twenty garments. Such an outfit would greatly minimize movement in the limbs and accentuate the delicate use of wrists and head. Postures evolved that would utilize the lines of the costume in the air design. The male also wore elaborate garments and headdresses, but the lower limbs were freer from heavy covering, and samurai swords were de rigueur, which aided in the development of strong lower-limb movements.

Both male and female feet were covered with *tabi* (tailored linen socks). From its earliest classicizing the dance was performed on a wooden floor, and this, together with the *tabi,* produced the controlled thud of the foot. Later the wooden platform of the stage was tuned in such a way that this same thud became one with the accompanying music.

Dancing and music were part of court ceremonials and festivals during this period and were presented with great delicacy and elegance. Thus, from its very beginnings the Japanese dance was a formal art, having been nurtured by the aristocracy in an age when the simplest acts of life, such as letter writing, were delicately formalized.

The earliest formal drama, the Noh play, was not founded until the fourteenth century during the Muromachi period. The Kabuki theater was born in the early seventeenth century during the Tokugawa period. Unlike aristocratic Noh, Kabuki was for the middle classes and as such absorbed elements of the folk dance (odori). It presented historical drama, musical play, comedy, and farce. It is interesting to note that Noh was performed exclusively by men; Kabuki originally (until 1629), largely by women.

The dance art of Japan is exhaustively documented and subject in all its facets to thoughtful regulations. There are techniques for the male and female walk, the back line of old or young, the kimono sleeve, and the pantomimic fan. So we find that the strongest influence on the Japanese dance arts was the social customs of the earlier periods of its perfecting: the Fujiwara, Kamakura, and Muromachi periods, into the Tokugawa period, which included treaties with America and Europe.

Let us now explore the movement origins of peoples living in the immense area south of the Sahara in Africa. An exhaustive application of our six-point plan would fill a small volume, for we are dealing with a tract of land twice as large as the United States that includes deserts, rain forests, mountains, and plains and is the home of dozens of varying tribes and hundreds of villages. Furthermore, what we might call material backgrounds differ widely. Yet there is one key to understanding and that is ecology. The intrinsic cultural values of the African people are an outgrowth of the continent itself. They are people for and of the land.

First, one must immediately disabuse one's mind of the notion that we are dealing with a primitive, stone-age culture. Great kingdoms have flourished in Africa, leaving behind them stone structures of fine workmanship, as witness the temple at Zimbabwe, erected when great kings controlled Rhodesia and Mozambique. Ghana was a great empire as early as 700 A.D. The city-state of Benin was creating bronze art in 1300. Yoruba organized the inland city-states in 1100, and the Shona ruled south of the Zambezi River for three hundred fifty years (1450–1800).

Bare feet are typical of Africa. Ancient bas-reliefs show warriors heavily armored and helmeted but with bare feet. Recent photographs of a great chief in intricate ceremonial garments and heavy jewelry show him with bare feet. So bare feet have conditioned the steps of the dances, and since these are generally performed out-of-doors, the rhythmic beat of the feet is almost noiseless and, due to the ground upon which they are danced, without the minute shadings of sound that grace dances such as the flamenco (shoes) or the Kathak (marble floor).

The amazing spine control prevalent in Africa is due to the physical conformation of the race. Thus a natural ability is refined into a brilliant technique, just as the natural balance and pliability of the Chinese have been developed into an exciting technique of the dance and the opera. Not only does the African spine often move in successions throughout a dance, but the head revolves rhythmically. One may even see the difficult *quebrada* turn that stars the Spanish technique.

But the strongest influence on the dance is a combination of social mores and religious beliefs, for these two are so interwoven that they cannot be considered separately. Both grew over the centuries out of conditions peculiar to the African continent. Over two thousand years ago a way of life was evolved that held that personal relationships were more important than material progress. Family solidarity reached out to embrace individual communities. This solidarity was the weapon of survival among the nomadic tribes, such as the Kinka of the southern Nile, who traveled great distances, taking their herds from watering places to feeding grounds as the seasons changed.

Man himself seemed a very small atom in the immensity of the land. Human life became precious, and warfare was carried on strictly according to conventions. An enemy was always left an opening of retreat, lest too much slaughter expend too many lives. Some tribes, such as the Tallensi of Ghana, declared war was sinful, and there was a good deal less intertribal killing than romantic novels would have us believe.

Religious beliefs were part and parcel of this solidarity. As the younger generation had looked to the older for guidance in life, so when an elder died, he was still a leader in spirit. In many tribes his body and possessions were preserved and wooden images carved of his spirit, so that he lived forever with his people. But he was not worshiped as a god, for Africans believe universally in the one God. This God rules the universe but is too distant and awesome to be annoyed with the lesser problems of the individual. So there are lesser gods, reached through the shaman or priestess, who will settle the small problems of mankind. It is not to the one God or to the lesser gods but to the essence of evil—the devil if you will— that living sacrifice is offered.

78

Islam, which is prevalent in the north of Africa, filtered into the south in the sixteenth century. But in the area below the Sahara the mores of Islam have been fitted into the ancient beliefs in the ancestors and the lesser gods.

Education also is a gift from the tribe elders. Young people learn morals, history and the craft of their fathers from their elders. The Nyakyusa of Tanzania have very strict views on sex life and hold *uwangalas,* formal discussions that the young may listen to as a form of education. In many tribes the young men are sent to a separate bachelor village for their advanced education, much as we would send a son to college.

Dance itself has a variety of motivations. As a ritual it is performed at funerals and puberty rites; it is done at the "history lessons," which recall, in choreographic form, great battles. There are dances in trance and in "possession."* And there are festival dances of pure gaiety and enthusiasm. But all are an expression of tribal patriotism or religious fervor.

Many Polynesian peoples have preserved their history through ancient chants. The Maoris sing that twelve tribes of Israel left Central Asia in the dawn of time. In a great migration certain tribes built the hanging gardens of Babylon and the pyramids of Egypt. Crossing the sea, some settled in America and begot the Mayan peoples and, further south, the Incas. After a stay at Easter Island they again moved westward to settle other South Sea islands, and some continued on to the Land of the Long White Cloud (New Zealand). It is an ancient tale refuted by some ethnologists. But there are traces of Sanskrit in the Maori language; the star of David (which is a cosmic design of the Hindus) can be found throughout the South Sea islands and among the Pueblo Indians; and in Hawaii gestures that mime the historical meles (chants) recall the classical *hasta mudras* of India.

A more recent "migration" of movement can be seen in tracing the influence of African dance on the dances of the Caribbean,

*See *Dance, Drums and Drama* by Deborah Bertonoff, privately published in Holon, Israel, 1976.

Brazil, and the United States, or the influence of the Spanish dance on Mexican and Peruvian expressions.

Ethnic techniques may also be analyzed according to Delsarte's trinal division, which I call the esoteric origins. Delsarte, as a base for his philosophy of expression, applies three psychological levels—the intellectual or spiritual, the emotive, and the vital. The anatomy and each part thereof may be divided into these three.

Division of the body as a whole:

1. The head: intellectual—spiritual
2. The torso: emotive
3. The limbs: vital

For immediate practical purposes I shall list only a few of the subdivisions of the Delsartian trinities.

1. Torso
   a. Intellectual: upper (thoracic)
   b. Emotive: center (epigastric)
   c. Vital: lower (abdominal)
2. Legs
   a. Intellectual: foot and ankle
   b. Emotive: calf and knee
   c. Vital: thigh and hip
3. Feet
   a. Intellectual: toes and ball
   b. Emotive: center arch
   c. Vital: heel
4. Arms
   a. Intellectual: hand
   b. Emotive: forearm
   c. Vital: upper arm
5. Hands
   a. Intellectual: fingers
   b. Emotive: palm
   c. Vital: thumb and heel of hand
6. Head
   a. Intellectual: forehead and eyes (frontal)

b. Emotive: nose and cheeks (buccal)
c. Vital: mouth and chin (genal)

As examples, let us apply this three-point plan to two ethnic dance arts—one Oriental and one Occidental—that are widely observed in the United States.

Even a superficial examination of one aspect of Spanish dance, the flamenco, will reveal the validity of this trinal division.

Flamenco is basically emotive and secondly vital. The attention of both executant and watcher is on the torso. The limbs move with great vitality but always to curve back toward the emotive torso. The entire torso is used and dominates all.

1. Within the dominating torso the emotive center (epigastric) is most important. The center body line is never "clouded" by clinging arms or loose-fitting costumes. The use of waist spirals is almost constant.

2. In the lower limbs the emotive calf and knee and the vital thigh and hip dominate. Leg lifts depart from the hip and are pulled back to the center force by the hip. The thigh is outlined in its lift by the *pantalon cenida,* or ruffled skirt. *Taconeo,* so typical of flamenco, is produced by the drive from the emotive calf and knee. Visually the foot is unimportant, and muscularly it is an instrument of the emotive lower leg.

3. In the foot itself it is again the emotive (center arch) and vital (heel) that dominate the whole. Most flamenco *taconeo* is produced by the heel and the flat (arch) of the foot. Only the more analytical floor contacts are done with the intellectual toes and ball. In the air, toes are not pointed but the emotive arch lifts.

4. The emotive and vital domination in the arms is quite obvious. The vital upper arm lifts away from the body to push and pull at the surrounding air. The emotive forearm curves back toward the shoulders, crossing the chest and sometimes half hiding the face. The hands move on a revolving forearm. It is not the hand itself that is important but the twist in the forearm and wrist.

5. Within the hand the emotive palm and vital thumb and heel dominate the intellectual fingers. The palm leads the fingers

and the fingers curve again into the palm. When the emotive forearm pushes outward, the fingers are led by the wrist and vital heel
of the hand. A spiral wrist moves the dominated fingers around
the vital thumb. *Palmas* (hand claps) are produced by the fingers
striking the emotive palm.

6. In examining the trilogy of the face, we find a delicate
balance among the intellectual (forehead and eyes), the emotive
(nose and cheeks), and the vital (mouth and chin). Here is the
eternally necessary balance, with the accent on the brows and eyes.
(Note that since the individual has been isolated for centuries by
social castes, the introspective, or intellectual, dominates the communal, or vital.)

In India the dance has been for many centuries a highly cul-
tivated art. Subject of attention from priest and pundit, it has an
established technique that leaves nothing to chance or the momen-
tary temperament of the performer. Unhampered by the characteristics of the dancer, in India we can observe, unobstructed, the
dance itself.

In this country the most widely known style is Bharata Natyam, one of the oldest and purest dance forms existing. In it the
intellectual (which is also the spiritual) dominates in every part of
the body. (It even demands an intellectual audience for full appreciation.)

Every part of the anatomy has its work, its techniques, its
dance function, but the head forever dominates the whole.

1. In the torso the thoracic section dominates. Shoulders
are used both rhythmically and pantomimically; the chest is high
the back flat. When the emotive center is used (as in *udvahita,* the
horizontal shift of the rib cage), it still remains visually subservient
to the lifting chest. (In some other styles of Indian dance, such as
Orissi, the vital, or abdominal, section is thrust to the side; but
again, this spine line is dominated by the chest lift. Movement as
such in the abdominal region has long ago been lost.)

2. In the legs the intellectual foot and ankle dominate. But
since physical movement is essentially vital, this vitality is under-
lined by the supporting thigh in the almost constant *demi-plié*

(note that hymns such as the *sloka* are performed without recourse to the lower limbs).

3. In foot techniques floor contacts are made by the use of the ball of the foot (intellectual) and the arch (emotive). When the heel is presented (*ancita*), the toe and arch are most evident.

4. In the classical arm carriage (*vartanam*) it is immediately apparent that the hands (intellectual) dominate the whole and that the emotive forearm is more important than the vital upper arm.

5. In the hand poses (*hasta mudras*) the trilogy of Delsarte could be a complete study, pose by pose, for each is an example of this trilogy. To show *man* the vital thumb is lifted from a closed fist. To show *protection* the emotive palm is held, facing forward, at the shoulder. *Soul* is indicated by the spiritual fingers opening like lotus petals from the vital joined wrists.

6. In the facial expression (*mukhaja*) of India Delsarte's philosophy is most apparent, for every possible tension has been studied and catalogued. In the Bharata Natyam style, which was originally exclusively feminine, the vital (mouth and chin) and emotive (nose and cheeks) are understated, while the intellectual (brows and eyes) are accented, being used as rhythmic accents in pure dance as well as for expressiveness in pantomimic dance. (Wherever the male principle dominates, the vital and emotive areas become more important.)

The true artist creates on instinct and leaves to the scientist the analysis of causes and results. Thus the study of typical racial body movements via the esoteric and exoteric origins herein set forth can serve the true artist only as a check or as a means of added strength. To the guru—the philosopher-teacher—of ethnic dance these plans are invaluable, for he can demand of the alien pupil a given impetus of movement style that will become an integral part of that pupil's physical technique and give him the racial characteristics hitherto considered impossible for the alien.

Needless to say, while perfect physical techniques can be taught, emanation is in the hands of God. But the student must not be dismayed by this truth, for all over the world essential life problems are the same—self-preservation, the pursuit of happiness, the search for God.

83

nine

Spanish Dance

To understand the changing face of any art it is necessary to know something of the social and political upheavals in the land of its birth. In Iberia the history of its peoples, the blood stream of Spain, is particularly important because the dance was made by and for the folk and did not become theater dance until the eighteenth century. Thus the characters and mores of many peoples have been absorbed into the Spanish dance as we know it today.

To begin with the incipience of dancing in Spain we must go very far backward in time. Indeed, we must go so far that we can only guess at the date as being somewhere between 35,000 and 15,000 B.C.

In the Aurignacian Period of Cro-Magnon Man we know that painters left records of what we suppose to be ceremonial dances on the walls of about twenty-five caves in Spain. These, then, were the earliest dancers of Spain—these shadowy tribesmen who painted and, no doubt, sang and danced their rituals.

The Phoenicians, who were traders rather than settlers, may have been in Spain as early as 2000 B.C. and were certainly not later than 1400 to 1100 B.C. The *danseas,* a round dance of Valencia, is of Phoenician origin, and it is sometimes claimed that the fandango of New Castile shows Phonecian influence.

During the Hellenic supremacy (circa 550 B.C.) Greece established colonies along the shores of Spain. Life as it was in the parent state was reproduced. Dionysiac and Silenic dances were undoubtedly performed. Castanets were used, as we can see from vases and figurines still existing. The counter line in the arms, the arched back and head, the spiral movements, all so characteristic of Spanish choreography, were also present in the Greek, as was the participation of the spectators by rhythmically clapping the hands (*jaleo*). The sardana of Catalonia is said to proceed from the pyrrhic and to derive from a primitive cult of sun worshipers. Some of the dances existing today that are believed to be of Greek origin are: the *baile de nyacras,* a Catalonian dance in which the dancers play oyster shells like castanets; *la folia,* a festival street dance of Valencia; *la danza de los huertanos,* a couple dance of Murcia; *ole gaditane* of Cadiz; *la danza prima* of Asturias; the *gallegada* and *muiñeira* of Galicia.

The great city-state of Carthage on the north coast of Africa was founded in 814 B.C. Carthaginians settled in southeastern Iberia, working the copper mines. They called this land Span, meaning hidden or remote land.

Rome annexed Spain in 201 B.C. and dominated the peninsula until 406 A.D. By 70 to 44 B.C. the southern districts had absorbed Roman ways, and their speech, literature, and gods were almost wholly Italian. Gadir (Cadiz), which was a center of art and culture during the Phoenician occupation, was the first city outside Italy to be granted both Roman personal franchise and Roman city rights.

In the Eternal City *las Andaluces delicias* were the dancers most adored by both artistic and social circles. The greatest among the Roman poets—Pliny, Silius Italicus, Petrone, Strabo and others —left to us enthusiastic strophes dedicated to these charming artists, and it was Telethusa, the *gaditana* celebrated in the epigrams of Martial, who served as model for the famous statue of the Callipygian Venus.

Roman domination in Spain was ended by the barbarian invasions. Vandals, Suebi, and Alans overran Roman Iberia. In 412 A.D. Rome asked for help from the Visigoths, who pushed the invading barbarians into the north of Spain. For over a century the confusion of wars among the several invaders dominated the peninsula, but in 531 the greater part of Iberia was united under a Gothic king. These Gothic kings embraced Catholicism and completely Christianized the land they ruled. Toledo was the capital during this era and was, with Saragossa and Seville, the center of culture and activity. Little is known of the art of this period, and we must wait for the coming of the Moors for information on the dance.

In 711 A.D. Arabs, Syrians, and Berbers invaded the Gothic kingdom through Gibraltar. Within seven years all of Iberia, with the exception of the Basque Provinces, Aragon, Navarre, and Asturias, was under Moorish rule. Under the caliphs Spain became the richest and most enlightened country in Europe.

During the caliphate of Córdoba dance and music performances under patronage were frequent. At these *leilas* song and dance carried the same title, and we find the *zambra, zorongo,* and *zarabanda* appearing.

But Spaniards were ill-content to play the part of the conquered. The reconquest of their land, begun about 722 A.D., took seven hundred years of fighting to achieve. The last caliphate, Granada, fell before Ferdinand and Isabella in 1492.

With the accession of the *Reyes Católicos* a renaissance began, and foremost among the protected arts was the dance. Masques and fiestas became the vogue, and from Spain came many of the court dances that were soon popular all over Europe: the *pavana, pasacalle, chacona,* and *zarabanda.*

Early in the seventeenth century productions were written using song, dance and dialogue. Presented at the palace of the Zarzuela (a hunting lodge of the king), the form soon became popular and is still known in Spain as the zarzuela.

The eighteenth century found Spain stripped of her power, prestige, and resources, yet this was the beginning of the golden age of the dance. A mode for the pastoral appeared and the court took to giving fiestas in the fields and woods. Folk dances were thus seen and admired by the elegant ladies and gentlemen, and straightway a new type of choreography came into being. The fandango, bolero, cachucha, and seguidilla were, in quick succession, danced by the court, taught in the dancing schools, and presented on the stage.

The seguidilla is very important in the history of Spanish dance, for it was, even more than the bolero, the model for various school or castanet dances that enriched the nineteenth century. It appeared in La Mancha (Castile) early in the eighteenth century but soon became so popular with the folk that it spread into several regions of Spain, with only the original title of *seguidilla manchega* changed (example: *seguidilla gallega* of Galicia). The *seguidilla sevillana* (of Seville) itself had many variations: *roncieras, espartero, la cava, corraleras,* and others. The basic choreography of these many forms of seguidillas did not change from district to district, but the character of performance was adapted to the style of the folk who danced it. The accompanying music and *coplas* also changed from district to district.

By the beginning of the nineteenth century the Spanish dance was well established in the theater of Spain. In 1834 Dolores Serral of the Royal Opera House of Madrid taught the cachucha to an Austrian named Fanny Elssler (1810-1884). This sultry dancer, leaping over the barriers of form to grasp the essential excitement of the Iberian art, surprised and inflamed all Europe with her interpretation of the cachucha and fandango.

Early in the twentieth century the *baile flamenco* appeared in the music halls of Spain. Until then little had been seen of the flamenco dance outside the barrios (gypsy quarters), save when a gypsy performed at street fairs to gather coppers. But the gypsy dancing for alien eyes is not the gypsy dancing for himself and his own. The Spanish professional determined to catch something of the controlled emotionalism that motivated the flamenco dance. In spite of the fact that the translated routines were set and the accompanying music was written, this new dance style was an immediate success. Old folk favorites began to introduce into their routines *taconeo* (heel beats) and other gypsy characteristics. This type of dance is called agitanado, and today there are few theater dances that are not agitanado.

The great teacher José Otero created dozens of dances that

he taught to his many professional students: *Ole Bujaque, Gracia de Sevilla, El Garrotin, Las Marianas, Las Guajiras, Fandanguillo,* and a host of others. The accompanying music, based on the tunes and rhythms of folk or flamenco music, was written by Sopena. This style of dance was in the repertory of every protagonist of Spanish dance, both concert and commercial, for the first two decades of the twentieth century.

For many centuries it had been assumed that to perform the Spanish dance the dancer must be Spanish-born. Even today there are those who stupidly accept this long-outmoded theory. This assumption brands the dance as solely a folk expression, yet the Spanish dance moved into the theater two centuries ago and rapidly grew into an international art form. Fanny Elssler performed both to the satisfaction of the Spaniard and the enthusiasm of the rest of the western world. Today many of the best-known protagonists of Spanish dance were born in the Americas. For the techniques can be learned by any healthy, dedicated dancer, while *duende* is God-given in any form of art. Not every dancer can be a Carmen Amaya, but then not every ballet dancer can be a Pavlova, not every modern dancer a Martha Graham.

Another error in too-general belief today is that all Spanish dance is flamenco. Nothing could be further from the truth, for the flamenco repertory is a very small percentage of the vast number of Spanish dances and only one of the forms of theater dance.

Forms of Spanish theater dance can be divided into six categories: regional, *escuela bolero*, Andalusian school, neoclassic, flamenco, and ballet (or dance-dramas).

Regional

The repertory of regional dances is so vast as to be mind-boggling. Earlier in this chapter we spoke of the ancient origins of many of them. There are thirteen regions in Spain plus the two insular regions, the Balearic and Canary islands. These regions break down into fifty-two provinces. Every province has its own typical dances.

Just to name and describe briefly this vast choreographic output would take two large volumes. Aurelio Capmany, who published such a work in 1931, writes that there are at least five hundred dances in Catalonia alone. The variety and elegance of the costumes are breathtaking. The music accompanying these dances presents differences in the very language in which it is sung, and the musical instruments vary from region to region. (Contrary to general foreign belief, castanets are *not* used throughout Spain.) Dances from the north of Spain differ from those of the south of Spain as distinctly as the Indian dance differs from the Japanese.

Relatively few of these regional dances have found their way to the stage. The most popular of regional theater dances is the *jota aragonesa.* Nearly every Spanish dancer has a number built on this dance. (Even the great flamenco dancer Escudero presented a jota on his concert program.) In detail it has often been distorted in transference to the stage. The folk do not leap about nearly so wildly as do the stage dancers. The oafish awkwardness, played for laughs, is not present in the folk form. And the Aragonese wears his castanets on the middle finger, not on the thumb, as do the Andalusians.

During the first two decades of this century other regional dances were incorporated into the school-dance repertory. Otero created a number called *Asturiana Soy;* Juan Martinez staged a dance from Castile; La Argentina also performed a dance from that region.

But it was La Argentinita (Encarnación López) who studied in every region of Spain and translated their dances to the stage in the form of *bosquejos.* These *bosquejos* (dance sketches) were a tremendous contribution to the theater dance, for not only were steps, costumes, and music traditional, but the basic character of the folk was treated with understanding and dignity.

La Argentinita was born in Buenos Aires of Castilian parentage in 1898. When she was four years old, her parents returned to Spain, where she began her study of the Spanish dance. From her first appearance in the music halls of Spain she was acclaimed by the public. In 1916 she toured the Latin-American countries. She made her Parisian debut in 1924. From 1939 until her death in 1945 she toured this country with her small company—herself; her sister Pilar López; a pianist; a guitarist; and a male dancer. On her first tour of the states her partner was Antonio de Triana. Later he was replaced by Federico Rey, and in 1941, Mr. Rey having been called to the armed forces, she engaged José Greco and Manolo Vargas.

Argentinita's contribution to the dance field is enormous. (her work in the ballet form will be treated in that section of this chapter.) She represented not only the neoclassic dance but also the ballets Español. She was the most eclectic of the Spanish dancers, being equally excellent in regional and flamenco. No other artist has handled so flawlessly the regional dance interpretations. The sardana, *charrada,* and *gallegada* in her capable hands became more than dances; they were a psychological study of the folk.

La Argentinita's partner, Federico Rey, was one of the first dancers to introduce the Basque dances to American audiences. His presentation of these dances was flawless and included choreography from both the Spanish and French Pyrenees.

The Valencian dances were introduced to the stage early in this century. The *Rhapsodia Valenciana* by Penella was used by some unknown choreographer as a setting for all the finest steps of the region. In this form it has become so popular on the stage that it has generally been accepted as traditional. More recently Nana Lorca, herself Valencian, has created elegant suites of Valencian dances.

In Madrid today there is a movement afoot to preserve the vast choreographic heritage of the regional dances. Societies of natives of the various regions have formed to write books and create films before these dances are lost to the ever-encroaching waves of modern living. For the student and fan of Spanish dance it must never be forgotten that the regional dance is the most Spanish of Spain.

The best known of regional dances is the sevillanas of Andalusia. This couple dance, which is an outgrowth of the seguidillas, has been the inspiration, if not the basis of the school and neoclassic forms.

But in the interest of chronology let us first take up the style of *escuela bolero.*

Escuela Bolero

By the end of the eighteenth century the dance in urban Spain was almost exclusively the bolero and the seguidilla. All classes, all ages danced and sang the *coplas* of these dances. Books were written that set forth the rules of conduct and execution of Iberian choreography. Pablo Minguét Irol and Carlo Blasis were setting the terminology and etiquette for the art. It was not until late in the nineteenth century that the *escuela bolero* style began to wane in popularity. Happily, it was never entirely lost, for the Pericet School has kept it alive and pure. Like the *nattuvanars* of India, the Pericet family has passed down the *escuela bolero* in its purity from generation to generation.

For the concert dancer the *escuela bolero* offers an exciting field of technique and inspiration. To the uninitiated it seems somewhat balletic in style, but any good ballet dancer, upon working with the bolero technique will find the very similarity frustrating; for the entire body line is different from ballet as is the *brazeo* (arm carriage). Hardest of all, toes must *not* be excessively pointed.

At present writing the Pericet classical form of teaching *escuela bolero* is in the hands of Luisa Pericet, the last of her family. She has entrusted her work to two Americans, José Fernández on the West Coast and Mariano Parra on the East Coast.

In its original form the bolero is a couple dance, but it can be performed *liso* (as a solo) or *robado* (a couple alternating solos). Important in it are the refinement of the regional *batterie* and the exciting air work of the ballet: *cuartas, lazos, emboteados, matalaranas, cabrioles.* Because of this technique it is generally danced in heelless slippers. Very rarely it is danced on point.

Andalusian School

Strictly speaking, the school dance includes all dances taught by a dancing master, from the pavane to routines of flamenco. However, the term is generally applied to the dances popular with theater dancers at the beginning of this century, which were founded on the style and general techniques of the regional sevillanas with some techniques of flamenco. As observed previously in this chapter, Otero created many of these dances. So popular did some of his creations become that they have been included in dance books and listed as "regional" dances of Andalusia.

In short, school dances are those that passed out of the folk to become theater pieces prior to the birth of the neoclassic and modern creative works for the stage. They are performed to music that might be called popular—melodies and rhythms taken from traditional sources and generally made into piano pieces for the sole purpose of dance accompaniment. Steps and movement designs for these dances are taken mostly from the seguidillas and Andalusian dances.

As a convenience to the dancing master, the limited teminology characteristic of the *escuela bolero* began to be enlarged to embrace Andalusian steps. In many cases this terminology referred to a combination of steps taken from a given folk dance. For instance, sevillanas refers to the six steps of the key combination of the folk sevillanas.

At the beginning of this century "presentation" dances were in demand. These dances opened a program and presented the artist in a very elaborate costume in which she did little more than walk around the stage playing castanets.

Few of us left remember the old school dances, but there are books in Spanish that give the steps and sometimes the music.

Obviously, it is impossible to name the hundreds of school dances that appeared during their greatest effulgence. Many believe this style is dying out since the growth of the neoclassic form. Yet many Spanish companies are still using the school dance, for any dance routine set to popular music is per se a school dance in both style and scope.

Neoclassic

The pioneer, some say the creator, of the Spanish neoclassic dance was La Argentina. Antonia Mercé (La Argentina) was born in Buenos Aires in 1888. Both her parents were ballet dancers, her father, Manuel Mercé, having been first dancer at the theater of Córdoba and both dancer and teacher at the Royal Opera House of Madrid. La Argentina made her debut as a ballet dancer at the opera of Madrid when she was nine and at eleven was a *première danseuse*. When she was fourteen, her father died, and she left the opera and began the study of Spanish dance. In her late teens she played the cafés of Spain and Paris, and a few years later, South America. But it was not until the end of the twenties that she was "discovered" in Paris and quickly became an international star. Concert engagements throughout Europe followed her Parisian successes, and for fifteen years thereafter she toured almost constantly. Beginning in 1928, she made six concert tours of the United States and three of South America, and was the first Spanish dancer to tour the Orient. On July 18, 1936, she died of a heart attack after watching a Basque festival in Bayonne, France.

La Argentina traveled without a company, her entire program being made up of solos to piano accompaniment. There were some school dances, such as the *Alegrías* from *The Land of Joy,* on her program, but it was in her interpretation of the classical Spanish composers (Albéniz, Falla, Turina, and others) that she was most brilliant. Previously it had been assumed that the great composers were to be listened to, not danced to. Even the Spanish dance aficionados were convinced she was wrong to use these compositions as dance accompaniment. What they did not understand was that she was not using this music as "dance accompaniment" but was making visual the spirit of the music. In this field she created her own dances, and this in itself took her compositions out of the school sphere, for the dances were not learned from a dancing master but were the pure emotional and choreographic creation of the performer. Her musical talent was unerring, and her control and musical understanding of the castanets remain unsurpassed.

La Argentina was tall and slim with fantastic charisma. Her very appearance lent a noble dignity to the Spanish dance. Yet the sensuality inherent in Spanish dance was present. It is said that the art she created was all her own and was based on the conviction that the dance must possess an inner content and communicate feeling if it is to endure. A few have criticized her flamenco as well as her folk dances, but this does not cancel out her creation of a new facet of Spanish dance. Nor does the fact that had she failed to do this work it would have been done by another in the inevitable evolution of the art. For no one can take away from her the glory that it was she who forced a skeptical world to respect the Spanish dance as a pure art form. She convinced all that the Spanish dance possesses a technique that, properly handled, need not lean on any other school but can stand alone, a classic structure as complete as ballet. She was the soul of all that was noblest in Spain.

With the renaissance of the Spanish dance in this new guise the choreography was no longer left to mood and chance but became a composition that must respect the triad of air design, floor design, and music design and embody the choreographic rules of contrast. The mood that inspires the neoclassic *estilo* must be felt at the first hearing of the music, the first impact of the idea, then, like the writing of a poem, the dance must be created in the clear memory of that mood. The intentions of the composer must be respected and the dancer must try to understand and perform the motivation that the composer intended in his themes. The castanets are not played ad libitum but are studied out in counterpoint, like a second voice to the melody. And at the service of all must stand a physical and mental knowledge of the technique as complete as is necessary to any great dancer and choreographer combined. The neoclassic Spanish dance moves as an infanta would move—with dignity and pride, whatever the other emotions may be. It uses the Spanish temperament to express moods as varied

and as deep as the human soul. The folk dance was born to amuse
the dancer. The cabaret dance was born to amuse the watcher.
But the neoclassic dance was born to inspire and to teach. The
foreigner, whether dancer or spectator, can never feel the full impact of the Spanish dance unless he makes a serious effort to probe
the true depth of the Spanish soul.

Flamenco

Now we come to the form of Spanish theater dance that is presently the most popular—flamenco. Indeed, it has become so popular
that many uninformed persons, including critics, students, and the
general public, believe it to be the only truly Spanish form of dance.
It is very important that this erroneous belief be exorcised, for
dance is an ephemeral art, and there is danger that the flamenco
will swallow up all other facets of the Spanish dance in the theater.
    The flamenco dance is the creation of the gypsies of Spain.
It is generally accepted that these gypsies are of East Indian origin
and were first brought out of India by Alexander the Great. Certainly there is much in their dance and music that recalls the dances
of northern India—the floor contacts, rhythms, turns. Some authorities say that one third of the words in the Romani language are
Sanskrit, and even a superficial study of Hindu music will disclose
similarities to the cante jondo (deep song) of the flamencos.
    In the middle of the fifteenth century there was a second
migration of gypsies into Spain. Vicente Escudero, in his book
Mi Baile, traces this migration through the north. Moving westward across Europe, probably through Russia and the Slavic countries, possibly through Germany and France, the Indian gypsies
kept to a code of racial purity and developed a pride that set them
"above all nations, a race of kings and queens."
    The Moors who conquered Andalusia were made up of three
different peoples: Berbers, Almohads, and Yemenite Arabs. The
Yemenites brought a very rich culture into Spain. They were devoted to the performing arts, and musicians, singers, and dancers
held high places in the courts of the caliphs. The great composer

96

Manuel de Falla has said that Moorish music was the strongest influence on the music of southern Spain.

Escudero claims that Miracielos (1800–1870) was the first to dance to guitar accompaniment. Prior to this time the dance was performed to a stick beaten on the ground to hold the *compas.* Probably because of the centuries of dancing to a percussive sound, the *jaleo* accompanying the flamenco dance had developed into an art itself. The *jaleo* consists of two types of hand claps—the *palma sordo* ("deaf," or soft) and the *palma seco* ("dry," or loud). To the rhythmic beat of palms, often in intricate cross rhythms, are added the occasional beat of heels by the *jaleadores* from their sitting positions and the cries of encouragement that are given only when the dancer has earned the approval of the *jaleo* circle. The well-known cry of *"Olé!"* may have come from the Arabic shout of "Allah!" with which the Arabic watcher approves the dancer. But the gypsy *"olé"* is generally sharp and loud, while the Arabic "Allah" is uttered in a long-drawn groan.

The evanescence of dance movements makes the certain tracing of origins extremely difficult. However, in spite of those enthusiasts who claim that flamenco dancing is an original and uncontaminated by any outside influence, it is only reasonable to deduce that during the Moorish domination three elements fused: the local Andalusian dance, the Muslim dance, and the gypsy dance.

Recorded history of the flamenco dance begins in 1842, with the beginning of the *cafe cantante.* At that time the repertory was relatively limited; women danced *alegrías* and its derivitives; men, *zapateados.* There was a sharply defined difference in the techniques of men and women. Women used their arms; men, their feet. The "dance of the arms" was highly feminine and passionate, while the *zapateo,* however simple, was full of strength and virility. This stylistic differentiation held for over half a century. La Cuenca (1860–1920) was the first woman to wear masculine clothes and dance in the masculine style. But the added brilliance of virtuoso *zapateo* was introduced by Antonio el de Bilbao and Carmen Amaya. In this country it was Amaya who set the style for women

97

to dance like men, and few noticed that as she matured, she too turned to the more feminine dance of the arms.

The use of castanets is also a recent innovation. As late as 1930 gypsies used castanets only in dances of folk origin (sevillanas, cachuchas), and men would not use them at all, considering them effeminate. Pastora Imperio says, "Today the *bailaoras* corrupt their defective hand and arm movements by using castanets and their lack of imagination and inspiration by prolonged footwork."*

There are very, very few *busnos* (foreigners) who have seen the pure flamenco dance, for this kinetic expression in its true form is performed in a state of "possession" (*duende*) akin to that of the dervishes. For a fee the traveler may see the flamencos dancing in barrios and cafés, but he will have to go many, many nights before a dancer (or a singer) will be "possessed" and express the true flamenco soul. What one generally sees—in barrio, café or concert hall —is theater flamenco. The artist who can consistantly give an honest reflection of true *duende* is rare and to be treasured.

The world of flamenco music and dance is in a continual state of flux. Many dances born in the barrios have been abandoned by the gypsies. Many songs that two decades past were not danced are new in the dancing repertory.

The true flamenco is not "routined" but improvised on a form, or *compas.* The *compas* is, roughly, the rhythm. But it is more than that, for whereas the actual time signatures of two dance forms may be identical, the accent within the rhythm will differ completely. The rhythm can be counted, but, make no mistake, it cannot truly be danced until the months of counting are behind one and the pulsation is felt emotionally.

The Ballets Español and Neoclassic Obra

The beginnings of the Spanish ballet lie in the zarzuelas that were popular in Spain in the middle of the eighteenth century. In the

*D. E. Pohren, quoted in *Lives and Legends of Flamenco*, Seville, Society of Spanish Studies, 1964, pages 220-221.

La Argentina (Antonia Mercé)
(about 1930). (Photo: Arnold Genthe)

La Argentinita (Encarnación López)
(about 1940). (Photo: H. Rand, Paris)

Mariano Parra and Ballets Espanol, flamenco, 1976.

Jota Aragonesa by the Ethnic Dance Arts Company, 1973.

Valenciana by the Ethnic Dance Arts Company, 1973.

La Meri and DiFalco in *Sevillanas*, 1951. (Photo: Preston Fleet)

La Meri with Balasaraswati and Ted Shawn. (Photo: Eugene Mitchell, Berkshire Eagle, Pittsfield, Massachusetts)

Uday Shankar in *Indra*.

Feminine costume of Kathakali (Srimathi Gina).

Bharata Natyam costume of the late 1930s.
(La Meri, 1940)

Ratilekha (Orissi style) at the Ethnic Dance Arts
Festival, 1973.

operettas that followed the zarzuelas, dances that were a part of the plot enriched every production. These dance scenes are comparable to those introduced into our own musical comedies in the forties, such as Jerome Robbins' Siamese ballet in *The King and I* and Agnes De Mille's danced scenes in *Oklahoma.* In the early thirties the ballets Español (danced stories) were seen throughout Europe. Juan Martinez (1896–1961) toured with his company. La Argentinita organized the Madrid Ballet with Federico Garcia Lorca and choreographed many fine works—*Las Calles de Cadiz, Cafe de Chinitas, El Amor Brujo.* La Argentina choreographed Duran's *El Fandango* (1927), Halffter's *Sonatina* (1928), Pittaluga's *La Romeria de los Cormider* (1933) and *Corrida de Fiesta* (1934), Falla's *El Amor Brujo* (1931), and Espla's *El Contrabandista* (1934).

But these ballets were all presented in Europe. In the States we had seen few purely Spanish ballets. True, libretto ballets had been presented by ballet companies, notably *The Three-Cornered Hat* (Falla) and *Capriccio Espagnol* (Rimsky-Korsakov). But inevitably these were in the ballet tradition and style with only somewhat distorted bits of Spanish technique superimposed upon them.

In 1943 La Argentinita choreographed *Pictures of Goya* for Ballet Theatre and the following year danced *El Amor Brujo* with the same company. Just before her death she staged a revival of *Cafe de Chinitas* at New York's Metropolitan Opera House. On this occasion she used dancers who were all trained in the Spanish technique.

In 1940 José Fernández choreographed *Goyescas* (Granados) for Ballet Theatre. But he was working with ballet dancers, and his *escuela bolero* techniques lost much in the transition to ballet style.

Carmelita Maracci choreographed *Guernica* at the Metropolitan during the early forties. But again, she had to use dancers trained in ballet.

We see, then, that the ballets Español in their true sense (i.e., choreographed with Spanish techniques) were seldom seen in this country prior to the forties. (How I deplore the term *ballet* in connection with ethnic dance! It leads to endless confusion. Why cannot some Spanish term be found such as *natya* for India's dramas and *zat pwe* for Burma's? *Baile dramatico? Fabula danzada?*) However, during the next decade we were privileged to see a number of outstanding "danced stories" created by choreographers in the Spanish genre; those of Ximenez-Vargas, Luisillo, and Roberto Iglesias are most memorable.

The full-length "ballet" is not to be confused with the *bosquejo*—the short, light danced sketch that was brought to its highest form by Argentinita. Every Spanish dance company presented one or two *bosquejos* on a program.

The neoclassic *obra* (work) is a composition for group using abstract dance (music visualization, if you will) to project a strong mood, generally with psychological overtones. In this wise it is comparable to the works of modern-dance choreographers. It does not tell a story, as does the ballet Español, but indicates a mental situation, an inner existence.

One of the earliest *obras* was La Argentinita's visualization of Ravel's *Bolero* (uncut). Using four dancers (La Argentinita, Pilar López, José Greco, and Manolo Vargas), it was first presented at Carnegie Hall in New York in the forties. Its success was instantaneous, and it will undoubtedly become an immortal work.

A number of fine Spanish-dance choreographers have visualized the classical music of Spain in the *obra* form. These works have been much appreciated abroad, but for some inexplicable reason in the States they are brushed off as "just another Spanish dance."

It must be remembered that a Spanish ballet or a Spanish work must use only Spanish techniques, else it is ballet or modern dance. The Spanish dance is a far older theater art than ballet and need not borrow movements from any other school. It can draw from four rich sources—*Escuela bolero*, flamenco, Andalusian and folk (in all its vast variety). Each of these has many steps and movements; each is an art in itself. True, it is not easy to find dancers adequately trained in the pure Spanish dance. True, the Iberian moods and music hold an endless fascination for the ballet and modern dancer. But only the choreographer who uses pure Spanish technique and dancers trained in that genre has the right to be termed Spanish. For Spanish dance is "the most ancient and the most noble of exotic dances."*

*André Levinson, *La Argentina,* Paris, Editions de Croniques du Jour, 1928, page 7.

ten

East Indian Dance

"India is a land and a people intoxicated with God," says Lin Yu-
tang in *The Wisdom of China and India.* The mystic form of
Indian religion has endowed all manifestations of the World Soul
(Brahma) with the visible attributes of symbolic man. Let is be
understood at the very outset that Hinduism is not polytheistic.
The many gods who personify world forces are not gods but the
manifold aspects of the one God. This mystic philosophy has been
the inspiration of the material presentation, through the visual arts,
of India's "intoxication."

Often represented is Siva in his aspect of Nataraja, Lord of
Dance. With his cosmic dance Nataraja sets the universe in rhythmic motion, and in this rhythm all things become and move. This
mystic concept has been growing for well over three thousand
years, and the student of Indian dance must have some understanding of this deep tradition if he would make himself a vessel and a
representative.

In the shadowy past before our annals of history an urban
civilization flourished in the Indus Valley in north India. As late
as 1922 archaeologists uncovered two great cities, Mohenjo-daro
and Harappa. These cities date back to about 2500 B.C., but beneath them were two other cities, the first of which was existing
in 3300 B.C. Who were these people who made copper pots and
gold and jade ornaments? They may have been the Dasas, or

Dasyus, who were the forefathers of the Dravidians of south India. Their way of life is revealed in their artifacts, but who they were remains a mystery.

Pinpointing dates in early Indian history is an impossible task, for it must be remembered that the calendar as we know it today was not in use three thousand years ago. Furthermore, there were several different calendars in early India. The arrival of the Aryans in India has been estimated as about 2000 B.C. The Aryans were a light-skinned, nomadic, and pastoral people who were most probably from Central Asia. These people created the Vedic philosophy and the Vedic hymns, the oldest religious writings in the world that are still considered sacred. The *Rig Veda,* probably composed between 1500 and 900 B.C., contains 1,028 hymns. The three later Vedas contain liturgical texts and sacrificial formulas. Within these texts were the beginning of the caste system and the concepts of karma (destiny) and transmigration. The priests were the most important and unassailable figures in the society.* Rita, the cosmic order, sustained the universe and regulated the conduct of men, and the god Varuna was guardian of rita.

Like the Hebrew Yahweh the one diety was nameless and was invoked by the syllable *aum.* This diety was depicted as an equilateral triangle. In the Hindu book *Nirukta* it is affirmed three times that there are three gods only and that these three designate one diety. This equilateral triangle superimposed upon another such triangle can be seen as the Hebrew Star of David. This same symbol, carrying the same significance, is used in Asia, the South Sea islands, and among the Pueblo Indians of America.

Of the namable Vedic gods representing the Nameless One, Varuna, god of the all-embracing sky, may be the oldest. Agni, god of fire, has been honored with more hymns than any other. Surya is the god of the sun, and Indra the god of the thunderbolt. Both Surya and Indra had man sons, for it is the sun and rain that propagate life.

---

*The priest was the mouth; the warriors were the arms; the farmer or merchant was the thighs; the servant was the feet.

There are many lesser gods and goddesses, such as Urmya (night), Usas (dawn), Prithvi (earth), Yama (god of the dead), Sarasvati (speech), Kubera (wealth) and Kama (love).

Brahmanism, the Hindu religion as we know it today, grew slowly and almost imperceptibly out of the Vedic tradition. Indeed, a Hindu is one who accepts the authority of the Vedas. But with man's inquiry into the Divine Plan, the simple Vedic gods of nature were slowly transformed into the Hindu gods of the Atman, or Infinite Soul. Rudra evolved into Siva. The Vedic Vishnu developed into a Hindu Vishnu. Prajapati became Brahma. Other Vedic gods became ancestral fathers and guardians of the world but were under the domination of the Trimurti, the holy trinity of Hinduism—Brahma, Vishnu, and Siva.

In representation each of the Trimurti has identifying characteristics. Brahma, the creator, is generally represented with three or four heads and four arms. His *vahanam* (vehicle) is the swan or goose. He carries the Vedas in two hands and in the other two, fire and the *cakra* (a disk, a weapon). His wife is Sarasvati.

Vishnu, the preserver, rides the Garuda, a mythical bird. He is of a blue color and has four arms with which he carries the conch (the call to battle), the *cakra,* the club (a weapon), and the lotus (symbol of eternal life). His wife is Lakshmi, goddess of good fortune. His *avataras* (incarnations) are the inspiration of sculpture, literature, and painting. He may be represented in any of these *avataras:* the fish, the tortoise, the boar (who saved the earth in the great flood), the man-lion, the dwarf, Parasurama (Rama with the Ax), Rama (hero of the *Ramayana*), Krishna, Buddha, and Kalkin (a savior on a white horse, yet to come). Of these perhaps the most beloved is Krishna, the blue god in his yellow garment, playing his flute.

Siva, the destroyer, rides on Nandi, the bull (worshiped in his own right). In appearance he has four arms and three eyes. In his hair he wears the moon, a serpent, and the Ganges. He carries a hind, a rattle, a small drum, and an ax or trident. His wife is Parvati (Mahadevi), who herself has many aspects; notable among these are Durga, goddess of battle, and Kali, goddess of death.

105

So many legends have grown around Siva that it is often difficult to recognize him. Some of the innumerable aspects of Siva are: the beneficent, the destructive, the meditating ascetic, and Lord of the Dance.

We have observed that the Vedas are among the earliest literature of mankind. The original work is the *Rig Veda* with its hymns. The second Veda is the *Yajur Veda,* which is the manual of the priesthood. Third is the *Sama Veda,* a collection of verses from the *Rig Veda* to be chanted by priests at rituals. Fourth is the *Atharva Veda,* which contains magical spells and incantations. The Brahmanas are ritualistic glosses on the Vedas. The Vedic hymns were revelations of the *risis* (inspired sages or seers).

The Brahmanas were composed by and for brahmans (priests). They are ritualistic and liturgical writings in prose and contain details of Vedic ceremonies and explanations of their origins and meanings. These Brahmanas are the oldest traditional narratives, linguistic explanations, and philosophic speculations still extant.

The Aranyakas (seventh century B.C.) are religious writings expounding the mystical sense of ceremonies.

The Upanishads (about 400 B.C.) consist of over a hundred works and contain the metaphysical inquiries that led to Hindu philosophy. Not concerned with ritual, they speculate, in prose and verse, on the nature of God. Monism (one god), karma (destiny), and transmigration are treated philosophically. Written over a period of three or four centuries, they exhibit great freedom of thought.

The Sutras (about 300 B.C.) are the rules or aphorisms that clarify the rituals, domestic rites, and conventional usages set forth in the Vedas.

The eighteen Puranas date from Gupta times onward, with eighteen Upapuranas, or subordinate works. Set forth in verse (four hundred thousand couplets), they are valuable records of the form of Hindu belief.

The Sastras (second or third century A.D.) are the holy codes or laws. The Dharma Sastras set forth religious and social behavior.

The earliest contains the code of Manu, upon which present-day Hinduism is based.

Three other literary works must be included in ancient brahman literature: the *Bhagavad-Gita,* "Song of the Lord," which is part of the *Mahabharata* (from unknown times to its compilation in 400 A.D.), a realistic tale of men and war, and the *Ramayana* (400 to 200 B.C.), the story of Rama and Sita. The last is a story of loyalties and has been used for centuries in the dance-dramas of Java, Thailand, Cambodia, and Burma.

I give a brief synopsis of the ever-popular *Ramayana.* Rama was the son of King Dasaratha of Kosala. When King Janaka of Videha offered his beautiful daughter, Sita, in marriage to the prince who could bend the king's war bow, many suitors tried, but none could shoot with the mighty weapon. Yet when Prince Rama drew on the bowstring, his strength was such that he broke the bow. So he won the princess. But Dasaratha's second queen, Kaikeyi, grew jealous of Rama's greatness and caused a rift in loyalties. To deal with the rift Rama put himself under banishment in the forest, taking with him only his wife and his brother Lakshmana. Their several adventures in the forest climaxed when the demon king Ravana became enamored of Sita and abducted her to his castle in Ceylon. Rama's efforts to rescue his wife were thwarted by the waters around the island until Hanuman, the monkey general, built a bridge. There follows a great war between good and evil, and Sita is finally saved. But Rama doubts the virtue of Sita after her long incarceration in Ravana's capital. Sita is justly angered by her husband's doubt and begs her mother, the Earth, to take her back. And so Sita returns to the earth that bore her, and Rama's "days of bliss are o'er."

It is written that *natya* (dance and drama) forms the fifth Veda. In the first chapter of the *Natya Sastra,* Bharata writes, "Thus, recalling all the Vedas, the Blessed Brahma framed the *Natya Veda* from the several parts of the Four Vedas as desired. From the *Rig Veda* he drew forth the words, from the *Sama Veda,* the singing, from the *Yajur Veda,* gesture, and from the *Atharva Veda,* the flavor."

107

The oldest available literature on dance is the *Natya Sastra*. This is a masterpiece on rules of dramaturgy, dealing with dance, drama, music, grammar, rhetoric, and rules for stage behavior. Although the *Natya Sastra* speaks of "others" who have written on the same subject, this treatise is the culmination of long tradition in the practice of dance and drama. The book is attributed to Bharata Muni. Muni (sage) is titular. Bharata is a common name in India, yet Vedanta Desikar, the Vaishnave philosopher, puts forth the theory that the name is an acrostic taken from *bhava* (mood), *raga* (melody), and *tala* (meter).

The actual period in which this much-discussed work was written has never been determined satisfactorily. As Bharata quotes Panini, it would indicate that the writing was post-Panini (fourth century B.C.). The literary form of the *Natya Sastra* is the *sloka* (verses in the form of eight-syllable lines), the chief meter used in Hindu epics. Authorities have variously guessed the date of writing, and nothing has been established firmly save that it was surely done before the Christian Era.

For the student of dance it is enough to know that in the *Natya Sastra* we have the oldest existing document on dance technique.

The *Natya Sastra* is divided into thirty-six chapters, and of these, twelve are devoted to dance. (Other chapters deal with the origins of *Natya* stage form, *purva-ranga* rites,* grammer and rhetoric, and music.) Most of the twelve chapters have been translated into English by authoritative Sanskrit scholars, and it is to these translations that the dancer turns for detailed information on this most ancient art.

Let us first look at *"Tandava Lakshanam,"* the fourth chapter of the *Natya Sastra,* as translated by Dr. B. V. Narayanaswami Naidu, Dr. P. Srinivasulu Naidu, and Dr. V. R. Pantulu. This

---

*Before all *natya* performances the *purva-ranga* is done. This is a worship formula dedicating the program to God and, in its entirety, takes an hour to perform. Many Hindu dancers on foreign soil still perform a shortened version of the *purva-ranga* before the curtain rises.

chapter describes the 108 *karanas* that comprise the basic postures of the dance. "A combination of the prescribed position (*sthana*), the gait (*chari*) and the hand pose (*nritta-hasta*) constitutes a *karana.*"

The 108 *karanas* are "illustrated" by bas-relief figures, one foot, two and a half inches tall, that decorate the *gopurams* (towers) of the temple of Siva at Chidambaram in south India. This temple is dedicated to Lord Siva and contains the *Nrtta Sabha* (Hall of Dance). Although the temple grew over a period of thirteen hundred years, it is generally conceded that the *Nrtta Sabha* is the oldest part.

"A single unit of action consists of two *karanas.* The *anga-haras* arise out of a combination of either two, three, or four of these units. In a *karana* the body as a whole is in one fixed position (or *sthana*), while in an *angahara* there is frequent change of *sthana.*" The *Natya Sastra* lists 32 *angharas.*

Further chapters in the *Natya Sastra* list all the fundamental actions of the body, its limbs and head. These listings vary somewhat from one authority to another, for over the centuries many pundits have written extensions of the original text of commentaries on same, then other, later writers have expounded on the commentaries. Further confusion is caused by translation from Sanskrit into Tamil, Telugu, and English. The scholar can speculate endlessly on the authenticity of each text (thereby writing still another commentary). For the active dancer I can only beg him to take my own listing, the selection of which is based on several authorities and which, over a fifty-year period, has proven successful in the teaching of Indian dance. The student must always remember that the following listing is a part of the ancient treatise on *natya* and comprises five chapters of that work.

9 *hasta prana* ("lives" of the hand: i.e., position, or movement)
34 *asamyuta* (single-hand positions)
An uncounted number of *samyuta* (positions of two hands)
17 *vartanam* (arm positions)
 8 *kaska rechaka* ("armpits," shoulders)
10 *kati rechaka* (waist)
 5 *vaska rechaka* (chest)

5 *akasa pada* (positions of the foot in the air)
7 *bhumya mandala pada* (positions of the foot on the floor)
15 *sthanaka stharam* (basic positions of the legs)
21 *bhumya chari* (steps)
22 *akasa chari* (leg movements in the air)
21 *gati* (gaits)
24 *bhramari* (turns)
9 *utplavana* (leaps)

Furthermore, the neck and face have been exhaustively catalogued.

20 *griva rechaka* (neck)
6 *puta* (eyelids)
7 *bhru rechaka* (eyebrows)
7 *nasa rechaka* (nose)
13 *asya rechaka* (mouth)
6 *cibuka rechaka* (chin)

Listings (and nomenclature) for the eyes are baffling in number and shading. There are:

9 *rasa dristi* (mood reflections)
8 *darsanas* (looks)
Asta dristi (glances) have been listed in numbers varying from 35 to 63.

For practical technical study I have cut down the expressions of the eye itself to:

9 *rasa dristi*
18 *asta dristi*
8 *darsanas*

There are nine *Rasas* (moods or sentiments)

Sringara (love)
Raudra (fury)
Veera (valor)
Hasya (laughter)
Karuna (pathos)
Vibhatsa (disgust)
Adbhuta (amazement)
Bhayanaka (fear)
Shanta (serenity)

The foregoing listing, properly learned and controlled, is sufficient for the dancer, at least during the first six years of study.

This scientific breakdown of the facial expression is so accurate that in demonstrations I have asked young students in technical terminology to respond with each separate feature of the face, one at a time, and the end result was a clearly expressed mood, although the students did not know what they had set out to express.

The study of *mukhaja* (facial muscles) would be a boon to many dancers who depend entirely on "instant" feeling to produce something other than a "dead pan" while dancing. Indeed, an intensive study of all the listed techniques would benefit any dancer of any style of dance, for over centuries India has discovered and listed every possible movement and posture of the body and face.

However, I hasten to add what is true of all theater arts: The technique, however brilliant, is nothing unless it is the vessel of *rasa* (flavor) and *bhava* (mood).

"Indian acting or dancing—the same word, *natya*, covers both ideas—is thus a deliberate art. Nothing is left to chance; the actor no more yields to the impulse of the moment in gesture than in the spoken word. When the curtain rises, indeed, it is too late to begin making a new work of art . . . so there is no reason why an accepted gesture-language (*angikabhinaya*) should be varied to set off advantageously the actor's personality. It is the action, not the actor, which is essential to dramatic art. Under these conditions, of course, there is no room for any amateur upon the stage; in fact, the amateur does not exist in Oriental art."*

The *Natya Sastra* divides dance as follows: *Marga* is sacred art; *desi,* secular entertainment; *lasya* is lyric,† *tandava,* heroic; *natya* is a full dance-drama; *nrtya* is expository dance; *nrtta,* pure

*A. K. Coomaraswamy, *The Mirror of Gesture,* New York, E. Weyhe, 1936, page 18.

†Nandikesvara states that in *tandava* the dancer stands to perform; in *lasya* she sits and gesticulates. An interesting parallel is that the ancient, sacred hulas of Hawaii were performed sitting and gesticulating. (See *Abbinaya-Darpanam,* published in Sanskrit; English translation by Metropolitan Publishing House Ltd., Calcutta—Calcutta Sanskrit Series No. V.)

111

dance; *vishama* is difficult dance; *laghu* is easy dance; *vikata,* clumsy (or bucolic) dance;* *svabhava-jah* is spontaneous dance. But only the gods can dance without regarding rules and techniques.

We may assume that the birth of Indic dance was the gestures used by the Vedic priests during ceremonies. Indeed, the great Sanskrit scholar Heinrich Zimmer, just before his untimely death, discovered and translated into English fifty-four hitherto unknown *hasta mudras* that were clearly defined as to be used only in religious rituals. Female dancers (*natas*) were an accepted part of the rituals (see the *Rig Veda,* Book 10, Hymns 18 and 94). These *natas* danced after funerals, danced at the house of a bride, danced at the Horse Sacrifice and the Soma Sacrifice. Many of these customs exist today, with the weight of three thousand years of tradition behind them.

Before regarding the styles of classical dance in India today, the student should take a brief look at the political and social history of that ancient land.

"Historic India is not a country. It is a culture, one of the oldest and most consistent on earth. That culture has been a contemporary to almost all civilizations. It existed, in nascent form, when the sun rose on Egypt's first kingdom in the fourth millennium B.C. Well developed, it was present when the sun sparkled on classical Greece in the fifth century B.C. and set on the British Empire in this century. The culture consists predominantly of a religion and a mode of living called Hinduism."†

Many migrating peoples followed the Aryans down into India through the Himalayas, and these were absorbed into the existing social structure, for the code of Manu permitted each to live in his own way without arousing rancor or bigotry. These immigrants included Indo-Europeans, Persians, Greeks, Scythians, Huns, Arabs, Turks, and Mongols.

During the Vedic Age, 1500 to 500 B.C., the Brahmanas and

---

*Folk dances and folk plays have also contributed to *natya.*

† Lucille Schulberg, *Historic India,* New York, Time-Life Books, 1968.

Upanishads were being composed, the Buddha (about 563 to 482 B.C.), was born in northern India, the kingdom of Magadha was established in northeastern India, and Darius I of Persia conquered northwest India.

Siddhartha Guatama (the Buddha) was born a rajah's son but forsook his birthright to seek "the Truth." He had studied Brahmanism but keenly felt the lack of altruism in these laws. For forty-five years he walked and taught his revelation of "the Way," "the Wheel of the Law." His sayings and sermons were written a century after his death: the Jatakas, part of one of the Pali canon. Although Buddhism has faded in India, it is still very strong in the Far East.

Alexander the Great reached India in 326 B.C. It is believed that his passage left an influence on the sculpture of India, and some say the draping of the sari was taken from the Greek.

The earliest of the three periods of glory in India was the Mauryan Empire (321 to 184 B.C.). Chandragupta Maurya was the empire's first ruler, and he learned much in tactics and government from Alexander. But it was Chandragupta's grandson, Asoka, who was one of the most enlightened rulers of history. Art and architecture flourished during his reign. He became a Buddhist, and much of the Mauryan sculpture still remaining in India has subject matter drawn from Buddhist themes.

During the period 200 B.C. to 300 A.D. many alien peoples followed Alexander into India. Greeks from Bactria established kingdoms in the Punjab and Indus Valley, and invaders came from Persia (Parthians), Bactria (Scythians), and Central Asia (Kushans). Yet literature and sculpture flourished, and in the southeast the great Pallava kingdom was established and lasted from the fourth to the end of the ninth century.

The Gupta Dynasty was the second period of glory. Founded by Chandragupta I, the Gupta Empire lasted nearly two hundred years (320 to 500 A.D.) and was destroyed by the second invasion of the White Huns. During the two centuries murals were painted in the Ajanta and Ellora caves in the Deccan; Sanskrit poetry and drama achieved their peak; Kalidasa, the great poet and dramatist, wrote

the drama *Sakuntala,* and Sudraka wrote *The Little Clay Cart*
(translations of both these dramas have been presented in the
West). Science did not lag behind. The decimal system was invented by an Indian mathematician, and Hindu astronomers knew
that the earth was round and revolved on its axis.

Six centuries were to elapse before the third period of glory,
the Muslim Empire. In the Deccan the Chalukyas established a
five hundred-year dynasty; the Chola Empire at Tanjore grew and
prospered; then the Vijayanagara kingdom was established and
was the last of the Hindu dynasties. In the north the Rajput kingdoms remained independent for about a thousand years and created
styles of writing and painting that still exist. In 712 A.D. Arabs conquered Sind and brought Islam to India. The Arabic Sind kingdoms
fell to the raids (1001 to 1027 A.D.) of the Muslim Turk Mahmud
of Ghazhi, who in turn was routed by other Turkish Muslims, who
established the Delhi sultanate. The Delhi sultanate lasted some
three hundred years and was finally conquered by Babur, the
founder of the Mogul dynasty.

Philosophy and literature flourished during this period (600
to 1500 A.D.) and elaborate temples were built. Also Marco Polo
visited (late thirteenth century), and Vasco da Gama landed at
Calicut seeking spices.

Akbar (1555-1606), the greatest of Mogul emperors, brought
unity and peace to northern India and conquered part of the
Deccan. The Mogul Empire lasted for nearly two centuries. During that period art and architecture flourished. The Mogul school
of miniature painting, which was based on the Persian form, became unique. Architecture also reached new heights. Great forts,
tombs, and even cities were built, including that gem of the world,
the Taj Mahal at Agra, built by the Emperor Shah Jahan (reigned
1628-1658) as a tomb for his beloved wife, Mumtaz Mahal.

The British, Dutch, and French East India Companies were
chartered early in the seventeenth century. Of these the British
soon became the strongest and absorbed the others. Over the
decades this trading company became a political force, and through
it the British weakened the rajahs of the separate states and, more

or less, united India into one country (1784). India achieved her independence in 1947, but at this time the predominantly Muslim areas were declared a separate nation, the Dominion of Pakistan. This partition resulted in bloody riots and the assassination of Mahatma Gandhi, who had lived by the law of passive resistance.

Even this brief look at the history of India will prepare the student to understand that for nearly four thousand years India was not one country but many kingdoms whose borders changed with wars and invasions. Because of the many foreign influxes in the north, it is obvious that the dance forms in the Deccan are today closer to the ancient art as expounded by Bharata.

Of the many forms of classical dance in India the best-known abroad is Bharata Natyam. This dance form is peculiar to the Deccan and is centered in Madras and Tanjore. Until as late as 1930 Bharata Natyam was performed exclusively by women —devadasis attached to the temple, the "brides of Siva." Thus the basic motivation is one of worship, and for this reason the dance embodies a certain austerity. If to the uninitiated the gesture songs and mimetic passages seem flirtatious, one must remember that the coquetry is directed toward the godhead and that the interplay is an allegorical one in which the human soul seeks oneness with God.

Technically, the dance is difficult and takes great strength. The deep *plié* and *demi-plié* that are maintained through long passages are characteristic and must be done with the ease of long practice. Movements and positions of the legs, arms, feet, shoulders, chest, waist, and all the muscles of the face are a part of the dance structure, which is based on a deep scientific study of human anatomy and its emotional expression. This does not mean that there is no possibility for the personal artistry of the dancer to shine through. The road to self-expression is a long one, yet comparison of two artists of this style will prove that Bharata Natyam is an excellent vehicle for the personality strong enough to achieve *bhava* and *rasa*.

Bharata Natyam repertory is made up of both pure dance and mimetic dance. In the latter the hands speak through a stylized gesture language made comprehensible of mood by the facial expression. In the pure-dance passages the floor contacts, or foot beats, are much prized, counter rhythms generally exciting applause from a native audience. The dance is architectonic in line and built choreographically on a series of *adavus,* or musical pharses, which build to a climax.

A classical program of Bharata Natyam is usually presented as follows:

1. *Alarippu:* An invocational dance, a short item made exciting by the alternations in rhythm. The performance of this dance dedicates the evening's program to Lord Siva.
2. *Jatisvaram:* A pure dance of technical brilliance.
3. *Sabdam:* This is *nrtya* (mimetic), but the pantomimic passages, which interpret a sacred legend or story, are alternated with brilliant interludes of *nrtta* (pure dance).
4. *Varnam:* A pantomimic interpretation of a *raga* (song), each verse interpreted with differing *hasta mudras* (hand postures) in three different ways, and each interpretation followed by a *tirmanam* (a passage of pure dance).
5. *Padam:* A more lyric *nrtya* interpretation of a song in *sringara rasa* (love mood). The song is repeated many times, and the dancer interprets the same words in many different ways.
6. *Tillana:* An item of pure dance depicting feminine allure and capriciousness.
7. *Sloka:* An unaccompanied chant interpreted entirely by the hands and face. The words are religious in character.

A recent addition to the repertory is *Natanam Adinar,* a brilliant *tandava* (heroic) number that demands great strength and technical skill.

Within the last forty years men of exceptional ability have begun to perform Bharata Natyam and have brought to this dance form a strength that has made for larger floor and air designs and a more direct theatrical appeal.

Kerala, lying along the southwest coast of India, has created and nurtures the unique dance-drama of Kathakali. Here are presented night-long dramas of epic tales from the Puranas, the

Mahabharata, and the *Ramayana.* Physical techniques are those of
Bharata's *Natya Sastra,* but all are done with great strength. The
mukhaja (facial techniques) are brought to the epitome of control,
the eyes being especially expressive. Arms move in wider design
and air work is used more than in any other form of Indian dance.

Pantomimic passages are laced with interludes of pure dance
(*kalasam*). Animals are depicted through movement—the elephant,
the peacock, the tiger, even a chariot drawn by galloping horses.
The clarity of representation is unequaled in the theaters of the
world.

Kathakali makeup is an art in itself and takes more than an
hour to apply to those in the leading roles. As in ancient Chinese
drama, the color as well as the design identify the character and his
emotional nature.

The elaborate costume features a skirt not unlike a large white
crinoline and a great, brightly painted headdress carved from wood.
A long-sleeved shirt and heavy jewelry adorn the torso.

The stories are all known to the spectators. It is not the un-
folding of the plot itself that holds the attention, but the matchless artistry of the actors and the aura of it all—the music and drum-
ming, the lighting from blazing pots of oil, the dedication of performer and watcher. All these lift one high above the mundanities
of everyday living, and one becomes a part of an epic life.

Kathakali has from time immemorial used an all-male cast,
female roles being taken by younger students in the school—a
schooling that takes twelve years to complete. More recently, in
performances outside Kerala, women have taken female roles.
And women of exceptional background have also been accepted
in the school.

Scenes from the Kathakali dramas have been presented in
western countries in recent years, but although the amazing techniques can be admired and applauded, the mystic aura is lost on
the western stage.

In the north of India the arts have been affected by the
several foreign invaders of that section. Immediately noticeable
is the lack of the withdrawn austerity that pervades the southern

forms. In the north the dance was not nurtured in the temple but in the palace, and the fact that its motivation is to delight the watcher rather than invoke a god gives it audience contact.

Kathak is the most popular of northern dance arts. Scholastic centers are Lucknow and Jaipur. Originally done by men, the dance is strong, bright, and extrovert. It begins with the *salami,* the greeting to the audience, and proceeds to alternate between rhythmic and mimetic passages. The mimed passages (*gaths*) often tell incidents in the life of the bucolic god Krishna, but it is not necessary to know the story or interpret the many hand gestures to enjoy these passages, for their lyric beauty is in pleasant contrast to the fast, beating rhythmic passages (*torahs*). The latter are based on a *bol,* or rhythmic sentence, on which the dancer improvises floor contacts in *tha* (slow speed) and *doon* (twice as fast as *tha*), the whole broken with spinning turns (*kathak* and *chakkara*) or with a cross-scan rhythm (*aadi laya*). Also present in the dance are passages of *thata,* a pose with rhythmic ornaments in the brows, eyes, neck, and shoulders. Stress is laid on the sound quality of floor contacts, the "thud" and the "slap" being accentuated by the fifty to one hundred ankle bells on each ankle. The long, full-skirted coat (*achkan*) worn enhances the many turns and is reminiscent of the Persian coat.

On the border of Burma in the state of Assam lies Manipur, whence comes another lovely and popular type of Indian dance, Manipuri. In the feminine form it is softer and more lyric in quality than the forms already mentioned and would seem at first glance to be easier of accomplishment. But unless the dancer is blessed with an exceptional natural grace and a gentle but persuasive personality, Manipuri is all but impossible. The movements of the lower body are unobtrusive. The arms are flowing and the hands flower and fold. Born of a deep religious faith and maintained by a strict discipline, the traditional repertory has survived the centuries relatively unchanged.

The *Lai Haroba* is a dance-drama presented annually for ten days in the month of May. Processions, circle dances, pantomimic passages, and duets invoke the gods and tell sacred legends.

There are many other dance-dramas in the classical repertory, of which we in America have seen only excerpts. Among the *tandava* dances exported to us the *pung cholam* is an item of great masculine virtuosity performed with a *mridanga* drum strapped to the waist in the manner of the Ceylonese dancer-drummers.

It is well to note here that when the great Rabindranath Tagore established his conservatory of the arts at Santiniketan, the form of dance he first incorporated into the curriculum was Manipuri.

We cannot leave our outline of Indian dance without mentioning, however briefly, several other forms that have more recently been brought to us by fine artists from India.

Orissi has been preserved in the state of Orissa, on the mid-eastern coast of India, since the seventh century A.D. Like Bharata Natyam, the technique is taken from the *Natya Sastra,* therefore from the ancient *karanas* as set forth by Bharata Muni. Repertory includes both *nrtta* and *nrtya* and a technique based on the *belis* (fundamental combinations; *karanas*) and *chalis* (rhythmic floor contacts). Although Orissi is basically akin to Bharata Natyam, it possesses a unique characteristic in the spine line—the *abhanga,* or S line of the spine, which is so typical of the ancient scuptured devadasis of ancient times.

The *chhau* masked dances of Saraikela (state of Bihar) are performed exclusively by males, are always masked, and are a part of religious rituals. Techniques are taken from the *Natya Sastra,* but the use of the lower limbs is more extended than in other classical Indian forms I have seen.

Mohini Attam is a classical dance form of Kerala, and although often performed by women, it partakes of many of the technical characteristics of Kathakali, such as the *motitam* (*plié* in wide second), the *abhinaya* (expressive mime), and the subject matter (legends and incidents from stories of Saivite interest).

These, then, are some of the many styles of Indian classical dance that we of the Occident have been privileged to see. The choreographic richness of the subcontinent is awe-inspiring. But in all its manifestations dance has been born of religion, and the dancer must never lose contact with the philosophic overtones of the item performed.

119

Recommended Reading

Aung, Maung Htin, *Burmese Drama.* Mysore City, India: Oxford University Press, 1937.

Bhavnani, Enakshi, *The Dance in India.* Bombay, India: Taraporevala, 1965.

Bonald, Caballero, *Andalusian Dances.* Barcelona, Spain: Imprenta Valez, 1959.

Bowers, Faubion, *Japanese Theatre.* New York: Hill & Wang, 1959.

Bowers, Faubion, *Theatre in the East.* New York: Thomas Nelson & Sons, 1956.

Brandon, James R., *Theater in Southeast Asia.* Cambridge, Mass.: Harvard University Press, 1967.

Buttree, Julia, *Rhythm of the Redman.* New York: A. S. Barnes, 1930.

Chujoy, Anatole, and P. W. Manchester, *The Dance Encyclopedia.* New York: Simon and Schuster, 1967.

Coomaraswamy, A. K., *Dance of Siva.* New York: Sunwise Turn, 1924.

Coomaraswamy, A. K., *The Mirror of Gesture.* New York: E. Weyhe, 1936.

Ellis, Havelock, *The Soul of Spain.* New York: Houghton-Mifflin, 1924.

Emerson, Nathaniel, *Unwritten Literature of Hawaii.* Washington, D.C.: Government Printing Office (Smithsonian), 1909.

Hawkridge, Emma, *Indian Gods and Kings.* Boston: Houghton-Mifflin, 1935.

Holt, Claire, *Dance Quest in the Celebes.* Paris: Maisonneuve, 1939.

121

Nandikesvara, *Abhinaya Darpana.* Calcutta, India: Metropolitan Publishers, 1934.

Pohren, D., *Art of Flamenco.* Jerez, Spain: Editorial Jerez Industrial, 1962.

Scott, A. C., *Introduction to Chinese Theatre.* Hong Kong: Donald Moore, 1958.

Shawn, Ted, *Every Little Movement. (A Book about François Delsarte.)* Pittsfield, Mass.: Eagle Press, 1954.

Shawn, Ted., *Gods Who Dance.* New York: E. P. Dutton, 1929.

Shawn, Ted., *Thirty-Three Years of American Dance.* Pittsfield, Mass.: Eagle Press, 1967.

Sorell, Walter, *The Dance Has Many Faces.* New York: World Publishing Co., 1951.

Tolentino, Francisca, *Philippine National Dances.* New York: Silver-Burdett, 1946.

Xarina, Zenia, *Classical Dances of the Orient.* New York: Crown Publishing Co., 1967.

Zoete, Beryl de, *Dance and Drama in Bali.* London: Faber & Faber, 1938.

Index